AF488545

Published by
Mind's Eye Publications
985 Deborah Avenue
Elgin, IL 60123-1918

Cover, Titling, and Interior Art and Illustration
by Paul "Mutartis" Boswell

ISBN: 979-8-9887924-2-0 [51795] / Trade Paperback
$17.95 US

What The Night Brings

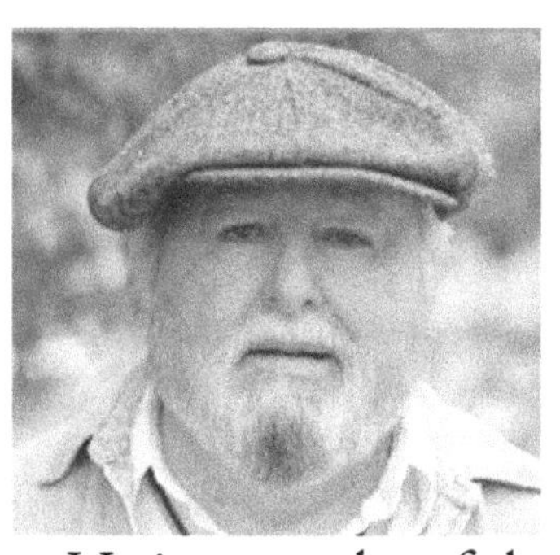 **FRANK COFFMAN** is a retired professor of college English, Creative Writing, and Journalism. His three previous collections of verse: *The Coven's Hornbook & Other Poems*, *Black Flames & Gleaming Shadows*, and *Eclipse of the Moon* have each received praise.

He is a membe of the Horror Writers Association and of the Science Fiction & Fantasy Poetry Association, in which his work has been nominated for both the Rhysling and Elgin Awards.

He is the founder and moderator of the Weird Poets Society Facebook group.

His collaboration with fellow speculative poet, Steven Withrow, *The Exorrcised Lyric* (Mind's Eye Publications, February 2021) offers two long narrative collaborations and 20 poems from each of the poets. In 2022, he published *Three Against the Dark,* his collection of occult detective stories.

This fourth large collection of his verse features more poems across the genres of the speculative, including especially the weird, horrific, and supernatural, but also inclusive of some science fictional and some more in the realm of folklore and legend.

As with the first three poetry collections, this book also includes some metapoetry, some *hommages,* and some more "traditional" verse—even some political poems
This tome also includes two large sections: *The The Kimi Xibabla* (an *epyllion* [mini-epic]) in the Cthuluvian vein and a 103-sonnet sequence over 72 titles, *What the Night Brings* in the tradition of the *Weird Tales* sonnet sequencers: Donald Wandrei, H. P. Lovecraft, and Robert E. Howard.

He lives in Elgin, Illinois, married to Connie. They are owned by two cats: Buffy (calico who slays vampires) and Binx (ghost chaser).

What the Night Brings

Frank
Coffman

Illustrations by
Mutartis Boswell

Dedication

For my great friend
and fellow bard of the speculative,
The Last Courtly Poet, and
Singer of Tales Atlantean—
Donald Sidney-Fryer

*A star shown on the
hour of our meeting.*

Ave! Sir Donald

List of llustrations by Mutartis Boswell

Table of Contents

What the Night Brings

& Other Sonnets

I
What the Night Brings

(a Scupham Sonnet in lesser asclepiads)

In the depths of the night, after the death of light,
When the sun is long set—then is *Their* time come round.
Then the veil between worlds, tenuous even by day,
May be crossed by vile hosts: souls who have debts to pay,
Horrid wights, demons dire. Evils most dread abound.
Ageless legends prevail, claiming the need for fright.

Out of cold, cosmic black, far beyond farthest star,
From the outermost depths, beings that ought not be
Would reclaim their old place, over our world would reign.
There are those who have sought, studied in tomes arcane
For lost secrets of Eld, spells that might set us free.
But the answers are not found in some cursed grimoire.

Though we may dread the time Night spreads her sable wings.
We should dread even more, far more—*What the Night Brings!*

2

II

Pericula Noctis

[**Dangers of the Night**]

[an English/Shakespearean -Sonnet in classical Alcmanics]

Deep in the Night there lurk perils most dire,
Portals gape wide when the pale moon holds sway.
New Moon is worst when no semblance of fire
Keeps out the dark from Black Stars—as in day
Cosmic Abysses are kept from our view.
Beings can cross when such gloom hides the tear;
Veil Between Worlds rends and *They* may pass through.
That is the time all Mankind should beware.
Dangers compound for those daring to go
Far from the relative safety of home,
Far from the places and people they know.
Nights become stranger the farther they roam.
  Many the reasons to fear well the Night,
  For there be *Things* that are far worse than Fright.

III
Unsafe Harbor
(a Couplet Sonnet)

It began slowly, but it wasn't long
Before she knew something was still quite wrong.
Things rearranged, the odd, weird nighttime noises—
And then she knew full well —there were voices!
Whispers within those sounds that broke her sleep,
That made her, even in daylight, begin to creep
With care around this house that she had hoped
Would be a refuge from It. She had vainly groped
For freedom from her demon, once exorcised
She'd thought. But no. She quickly realized
That it had followed! She'd thought a thousand miles
Were distance enough. But demons have their wiles.
Once more she'd seek to be exorcised and blessed…
…But the priests found her, irretrievably possessed.

IV
The Mahwot
[a creature from the Belgian Bestiary]

A river creature with a gaping mouth,
A terror to the children of the Ardennes,
Back and forth from Liege to the South
And back up North it goes to Revin.
Amphibious, it runs on the river's bed,
Scourge of the Meuse it seeks out prey.
Children are warned of this beast to dread,
Warned never too near the water to stray.

It's rare when it leaves its watery home,
But, if it's seen on the land to roam,
It portends tragedy. Mother's use its fear,
"You be good, for I think the Mahwat's near!
I'll call for him!" And their fear is real—
Not wishing to be the Mahwot's next meal!

V
Leitmotif
(an Interlocking Rubáiyát Sonnet)

Somehow—within his mind—he heard it clear;
Shockingly loud, since no one else was near.
It sounded like some inner grand piano
Banging those notes out in his head! The Fear
Began with the first repeat. He could not know
At first that he was cursed. The tune would grow
To a crescendo and then slowly wane
To a mere "ear worm." But that awful flow
Was ceaseless! Over, over, again, again!
He tried to "live over it" but that horrid strain
Was unrelenting, would not let him sleep.
Knowing at last he was no longer sane,
He opened the kitchen drawer where he would keep
The knives… plunged one into his ear full deep.

VI
Moons of Doom
(a Clogyrnach Sonnet—invented form)

When full moon skuds through cloudy sky,
'Tis then that someone's doomed to die.
Then the werewolf prowls.
'Midst the hoot of owls
Come its howls. It is nigh!

Most dreadful is the man-wolf's bite.
If you don't die that very night,
Your fate—something worse!
You will own the curse—
To rehearse that dire plight:

Each month, at time of plenilune,
Your human shape will change
Into a Thing most strange,
Fated to range 'neath round moon.

VII

The time of Old Samhain draws nigh

(Sonnet in Ancient Egyptian "Thought Couplets")

The time of Old Samhain draws nigh;
The aging year wanes toward the Long Night.
Rites of the ancient Celts are still practiced;
In secret groves and dark dells old religion holds sway.
Most ignorant mortals today call it "Halloween,"
That day before the day of All Saints, "All Hallows Eve."
The veil, a web of sheerest gossamer, is rent;
The fabric between Our world and Theirs is torn.

Meanwhile, a mockery of the horrors that truly spread abroad,
The unbelieving living costume themselves and feign to frighten;
They threaten "tricks," not kenning how near is true Terror;
Yet some will discover how real are legends of the Dark.
And still, in mystic rites and magic places, the chants rise;
The warding sacrifices continue beneath cold autumn skies.

VIII
The Lorelei
[a German Legend]

A huge and jagged cliff of dark, grim slate
Rises above the Rhine, cutting the sky.
And sailing men have found their place to die
Beneath that "Murmuring Rock," meeting their fate.
For She croons there atop that craggy height
And, with her singing, lures them to the rocks
With silver sibilant song and golden flowing locks—
Breaking ships…and the silence of the night.

The Lorelei lurks there and weaves a message
To all unwary sailors who dare that passage.
Who know the legend pray the Saints deliver
Them from her beck and call, from that dire shore.
Still, many are enthralled, steer toward Death's Door,
And meet the rocks and doom beneath the river.

IX
Power Outage

His first reaction was far short of outrage
"Situation normal…" he even skipped the rest
Of the quote in thought. "Well, Damn! Another outage."
They seemed more frequent lately." And the rest
Of his block was dark he saw as he looked out.
There was an odd—no, a weird?—color in the sky
He"d never seen before. Then he heard a shout
Just down the street. And then debris whisked by
His view. And then the screams of terror began!
Soon after, a strange yellow filled the room.
His front door burst open wide. This was no man!
It raised one of six arms. He saw his doom
But briefly, as the hideous alien beast
Dissolved his essence.

                    They had power at least.

X
Nearing All Hallows
(Middle English "Thirteener")

Now All Hallows Eve is near—
By its pagan name "Samhain."   [pron. sa-wen]
Autumn reigns, and chill and drear
Nights darken. The Veil grows thin
Between two worlds—That of Fear,
This of Ours. Since Time began
That Wall through which we may peer
On rare times…it falls!—and then—
Evils break free!
Halloween is one such time.
Though we mock with foolish mime
Horrors coming from that clime,
Fiends from *That Zone* you may see!

XI
Spectral Sentences

"All Hallow's Eve. Here is a boy who mums
Our kind—his grim mask shows a frozen scream.
Another wears a stark white sheet; eyes gleam
From scissored holes. And look—another comes
With pallid, 'blood'-flecked face. The night wind numbs
These mortal shivering things, yet still they seem
To be enjoying this charade. They do not deem
They will encounter us one day. True Phantoms!

"But now!— their souls are marked to see *Our Realm*.
I'll leave to you the sheeted one—to you, the masked.
That lad with false-blood face will meet my ultimate Terror.
Take all the time you wish to gradually overwhelm
Their spirits. But remember—you are tasked!
Deathly white, true-bloody—when mine meets me *There*.

XII
Monstrous Meetings

"See how these children mock us, avatars
Of we who would confound their foolish play
With horror if they met *US* 'neath these stars,'"
The Dead Undead vampiric wight did say.
    "Truly, they are quite foolish This Night to tread;
Full moon, by chance. I will choose one to slay,"
The man-wolf answered. "His joy will turn to dread
When he beholds these fangs ere break of day."
    "Yes. Must know the truth," said the assembled man,
Reanimated by the force of lightning's might.
The three moved forward. The children screamed and ran…
But three young souls returned not home that night.
    One gave his blood, One a beast's maw sated,
    One was crushed from life. Misguided play thus fated.

XIII
"He's Gonna Find Out!"

"…he sees you when you're sleeping,
He knows when you're awake,
He knows if you've been bad…"

With cloven hooves and long, curved horns on head—
Below a goat, but above a manlike shape—
If you're marked down into his Book of Dread,
For you there is no true hope of escape.
On the fifth of December he will come around,
In search of children who've been very bad.
If any trace of wickedness is found,
Then it will be too late to wish you had
Been kinder, friendly, loving, doing good.

On Christmas he'll return with chains and whips
Of birch twigs and a sack. It's understood
Whipping's the best to hope for. If he slips
You into the sack it's known full well
Cruel Krampus then will carry you to Hell!

XIV
The Clingers

There are souls, disembodied, and their fate
("Denuded" from their flesh, due to foul sins
So enormous that they cannot transmigrate)
To cleave to people—so the curse begins.
People whose secret wrongs have opened the Door
To let "the Clinger" in. It makes them crazed.
The thing can use their mouth to speak. Before
They are aware, their body is amazed
To find two souls within! And one a Demon vile.
No peace for such a victim. And the schism
Between the cursed one and the *Dybbuk* soul
Grows. And the only answer—Exorcism.
    At best, into an object the Terror will go—
    At worst, to another human—a transferred woe.

XV
Pareidolia?
(a Scupham Sonnet)

"After I saw the face in the paneled wall,
Eyes closed, mouth set in a horrid, evil grin,
At first, I felt no real dismay or fear,
Although uneasy—since it seemed so clear!
But slowly, very slowly dark thoughts began to win,
The Face began my senses to appall.
    "I told my doctor that his office paneling
Showed clearly a demon's visage, a curséd face."
I said, 'It's there man! Don't you see!?"
He looked, he even stared, then said to me:
'I want you to keep a journal to replace
Your thoughts that ramble in delusional channeling.'
  "I've broken in and must look. No escape!
   See now! The eyes! Wide open! Fanged mouth agape!"

XVI
Beyond the Borgo Pass
[recovered jottings from the journal of
R. M. Renfield, solicitor]
(a Couplet Sonnet)

"Regarding this trip, I have great expectations.
I've handled several sales of grand locations,
But Carfax Abbey will be my true 'crown jewel!'
First time to see Romania. As a rule,
My work near London keeps me busy enough.
This coach ride is a bit thrilling. The road is rough.
Besides the depth of night, thick mists encroach.
I leaned out. A bat almost seems to lead our coach!

. . .

"We've stopped. Ah! here is my host's coach and pair.
A crossroads. My driver hurried to leave me here?
He said, 'God be with you.' Not the short 'Goodbye.'
And then he crossed himself. I wonder why?

. . .

"I must say the howls of wolves gave me a fright.
My host calls them 'The Children of the Night....'"

XVII
Cosmic Quandaries
(a nonce sonnet using slant rhymes)

Beholding "The Bowl of Night" thoughts must intrude.
Mickle myriads of stars! The vast infinitude
Of the deep sky; it seems a gleaming dome.
That's but a Necessary Trick upon our eyes,
The truth too awesome for our wild surmise.
"Is This or Somewhere-Out-There our True Home?"
    Or when we see that Burning Ship, the Sun,
Wending its way adown the dimming Day,
And think upon The Race—long or short run:
Oblivion? Heaven? None have returned to say.
The Far Lands? The Islands of the Blessed?
The Final Grade on Life, The Teacher's test?
The Question puzzles none of us, at last:
"What lies Beyond that Rim, far west of West?"

XVIII
The Doorway

"ina qabri ba-a-bi iptu-uma-a inakitiba-a-bi iptetu-u"
[Sumerian, from *The UDUG HUL**]
"In the tomb, they opened a doorway to the Netherworld."

"From Uruk, the site was several miles to the east.
A wild-wind Shamal had cleared the ancient stone,
Revealing an entrance to whose tomb? As yet unknown.
Two days after that great dust-storm had ceased—
Despite the warnings of that Zoroastrian priest—
Our team went quickly to that House of Bone.
   "We found more cautions on the lintel stone
In Early Sumerian.…They told that an Evil Beast
Had been sealed in behind a black stone door.
Indeed the "tomb" was but a hollow vault.
No mortal remains or funerary gear
Are in that chamber, etched on walls and floor
With horrid charms.
          "The growling made us halt,
Fill in, and rebury that place of Primeval Fear."

[**The Udug Hul*: tablets of text containing chants or charms to exorcise
the "Evil Udug"—literally "Udug Evil" or "Demon of Evil"])

XIX
Leannan Sídhe
[from the final notebook of Liam Ó Súilleabháin]
(an Irish Ochtfochlach Sonnet—an invented form)

From that first time she visited me,
I knew what my destiny would be:
My muse was of the Leannan Sídhe,
One of the "people of the barrows."
All of my poetry has been fired
By this Wraith whom I have most desired;
Her weird "love"—accepted—has inspired
All my works. But my life now narrows.

I knew the price when I let her in—
And loved her well in my secret sin—
But now my body and mind begin
To pay for her sweet motivations!
My life force, my very soul grows thin…
Drained Life! has imbued my creations.

20

XX
A Cabin in the Wood
(a sonnet sequence)

1

The legends had it that a curséd cabin lay
Deep in the woodland near the forsaken town.
He thought to explore, to cast such fables down.
The ways of superstition were at play,
As he knew well. His work had been to dispel
The stuff of legend—mere folktales of the dark,
The fires of folly kindled by the spark
That ever glowed in Man's self-created Hell.

That eldritch cottage they said was "…beyond weird!"
Among those few who'd seen it, one old man
Said, "No place has seared my mind more foully than
That cabin; no place more fully to be feared!
I saw it but briefly, but I had to turn and run.
It's as if the Laws of Nature are undone!"

2

"It's shaped as if the builder had no plan,"
Another said, of those few who'd drawn near.
"And very strange…though some have seen it clear,
To remember or describe it—no one can."
"I've heard tales of two who dared to go inside,"
The old one added, "but I warn you, Sir,
No telling what awful Evil you might stir!
Only one came back. He was insane—then died!"

The folklorist noted all this in his journal.
And, venturing forth the following day at dawn
To seek the place whose wooden walls were thrawn,
Despite the warnings "Something…worse than infernal
Dwells in that cabin. Please, stranger, do not go!"
But the truth behind these tales he had to know.

3

He found the place, long-hidden in the wood,
By merest chance. The glint off one window
Shot straight to his eye as sunset—red as blood—
Brought down the day. There was no way to know
That cabin—lost in tangles of weird vines,
All but concealed through angles of odd trees—
Was built along strange non-Euclidean lines.
Contours impossible! His blood began to freeze.

But when he went through that strange, ill-shapen door,
The sight, though dimly lit, amazed his thought:
The angles, dimensions, windows, walls, and floor
Were skewed in impossible lines! "No 'real' things ought
To look like this!" And, most abhorrent, the room inside
Was far, far larger than the shape outside!

That cabin—lost in tangles of weird vines,
All but concealed through angles of odd trees—
Was built along strange non-Euclidean lines.
Contours impossible!

4

He lit a torch. He'd come prepared at least
For darkness—but not the kind he'd find.
Crossing the odd-slant floor, his fear increased,
As he neared an inner door. What might lay behind
That portal filled him with dread. A great unease
Came over him as he thought "I have to go.
I've come to this horrid place. I have to know!"
He entered—and then he knew!....
                                    Grim congeries
Of ghastly things, a cumulus of Terror,
Huge heaps of bones and gore and vile things slithering
His torch revealed. Great God! The Evil there
Was palpable! He sensed his sanity withering.
In horror, he knew, "I'll never leave this place!"
Then he beheld the dwelling Demon's face!

XXI
Dweller in the Hidden Chamber
[The Great Pyramid, Giza]
(a 4-6-4 Sonnet — invented form)

Ah! They have detected my cell as last!
Compared to the millennia I have lain in wait—
Now but a short time before they delve some gate,
Some doorway to this place that has held me fast.

Far blacker than the blackness of my tomb
Have grown my Dark Spirit and my Evil Will.
They hoped these walls of lead, these tons of stone
Would keep them safe—perhaps would be my doom!
But I, Apep-Asfet, Chaos, Champion of Evil,
Have grown my plans for eons here alone.

They have forgotten why this hidden hall
Was formed, this crypt of horror without a portal.
Now dead are all the priests and mages. No mortal
Can stop the Terror, the Darkness that will befall.

XXII
Gargoyle Thoughts
(a Quatrain-Couplet Blend Sonnet—invented form)

I am not formed as these who walk below,
But formed *by* them who have much quicker brains.
They can't imagine that I could observe-or know!
They find me interesting, but useful only when rains
Are gathered and spewed from my grim, malformed maw.
To believe I think breaks every natural law
They hold as "Truth." Though my cold, hollow heart
Will never feel their kind's hot coursing blood,
Yet still I know my folk and play a part—
To weather all weathers, bright day or snow or flood.
The calm, dry days they love bring me the pain
Of thirst. But, ever patient, I pray for rain.
Though slow of wit, at least I know my purpose.
Many who move below me settle for less.

XXIII
The Omega Variant
(an irregular sonnet-15 lines)

At Omicron, we thought we had it stopped,
But Omicron transmuted into Pi,
Then re-evolved itself as millions dropped,
Then billions by the time we got to Phi.
Another "breakthrough" gave us hope through Chi,
Yet still the Horror spread, growing more strong,
'Til few were left who claimed the Science wrong.
The remnant, with one universal Psi,
Now knew our time remaining wasn't long.

Inevitably, Omega meant our doom!
Though that was sealed already: climate change,
Volcanoes, earthquakes, tsunami, famine, flood,
Hurricanes, fires, Chaos…that last not really strange.
Finally, we knew we truly shared the blood
With all those hominids long-resting in the tomb.

XXIV
The Tommyknockers
(two Cornish Sonnets)

1

All delvers in the deep, dark mines of tin
Know that strange sprites are with them in the gloom.
The Tommyknockers dwell those depths within,
Souls of lost miners whom the toil has claimed,
Spirits of those who met a dismal doom—
Some known, but many who remain unnamed.

Know that the Knockers are both boon and bane.
The knocks can lead on to a rich new place,
Can lure the diggers to a full new vein.
But they must stay attentive to the sound.
For, if the knocks are loud, with frenzied pace,
A cave-in's likely. And many won't be found.

All delvers in the deep, dark mines of tin
Know that the Knockers are both boon and bane.

2

A strange, weird lot, these tiny, wizened sprites—
Just two feet tall, long-armed, but with huge head,
Gnomes thriving in the mine's eternal nights.
To keep them happy, the miners know to throw
Last morsels or their final crust of bread
As gifts to keep them safe from harm below.

Benevolent yet mischievous they be,
And they will pilfer food and miners' gear.
Unguarded lunch, or—if they're on a spree—
Chiefly helmets and head-lamps they will take,
For Knockers' "noggins" are man-size or near.
So, delvers guard their wares—for their own sake.

A strange, weird lot, these tiny, wizened sprites—
Benevolent, yet mischievous they be.

XXV
The Spriggans
(a Cornish Sonnet)

In Old Cornwall there dwell a wicked race—
The Spriggans! These weird wights are wont to dwell
In ruins, cairns, barrows and any place
Where treasure's buried. You had best beware
These ghosts of giants, ugly fiends most fell.
Of evil mischief they do their full share.

Supernatural creatures you should dread,
First glance, they seem old, wizened, grotesque men,
Small for their ghost—but with large, childlike head!
They can cause storms, steal cattle, damage homes…
Much worse, by night they invade dwellings…then
A Changling found in crib when morning comes.

In Old Cornwall there dwell a wicked race—
Supernatural creatures you should dread.

The Spriggans

XXVI
Joan-the-Wad* & Jack-the-Lantern
(a sonnet using Cornish Type II Stanzas—
variant octave, normal sestet)

Jack-the-lantern, Joan-the-wad,
That tickled the maid and made her mad,
Light me home, the weather's bad!.
— Northall, G.F. (1892).*English Folk Rhymes*

Queen of Pixies, Joan-the-Wad,
Will tempt those who walk abroad
To their peril o'er the moor.
Jack-Lantern too leads astray
Those who tread past end of day.
Both these whispy wights will lure
Travelers to lose their way,
Lead to danger—that is sure!

From the dolmen and stone ring,
Great mischiefs the Pixies bring.
Not the least their King and Queen,
Jack and Joan with luring light
Will betray you in the night.
Ne'er again might you be seen.

[* In Cornish, a "wad" is a torch
or a bundle of straw (of course,
from which torches can be made).]

XXVII
The Korrigans

[a Breton Sonnet—invented form
on legendary Breton creatures]

Not of mischievous gnome I write;
No dwarf or fairy this fey sprite,
But those who in our waters dwell,
In springs and rivers who will lure,
Song-enthralled, men to death most sure—
To be drowned by these sirens fell.

These fiends, white-robed, with flowing hair
By dusk or night seem beauties rare.
But by day, eyes of red, hair white,
Wrinkled crones from light they will hide,
Cloaking until the day has died,
Waiting to deal death in the night.

At Full Moon, these pagan sprites dance round fount or rill.
On Samhain 'neath dolmens they lurk, waiting to kill.

The Korrigans

XXVIII

Gwyllion
["Spirits of the Gloaming,"
"Night Wanderers"]
[pronounced goych-yon
with "ch" as in Scottish "loch"—
from Welsh *gwyll* : '<u>goych</u>' "twilight/gloaming"]
(a Hir a Thoddaid Sonnet—invented form)

After darkness falls and through the long night
Ghastly spirits wander past the gloaming.
The Gwyllion, ghostly hags, are wights of fright.
After twilight, you may meet one roaming
The moonlit pathway of a deep black wood.
Beware! She could lead you far astray—
Astray to what will likely be your doom.
These evil wanderers will betray
Whoso would go the mountain roads of Wales,
The Gwyllion haunt those trails in dark or gloom
Of mist. And one may loose all hope, all chance
To find one's way. Sense of direction fails.
    Your only hope—show a knife's shining blade
    That be your aid— the one fear they know.

XXIX
I See Too Much:
A Clairvoyant's Complaint

My gift…my curse is that I see too much—
Not with my eyes, but with my "inner sight."
It haunts my days and wakes me in the night.
My vivid visions…always too late! Such
Is a source of agony, for they tend—
Though starkly clear, to show a scene of gore—
To show a tragedy, some poor soul's end.
Too late is worse than never, so before
My bane beholds another wretched death
That can't be thwarted—I will end this woe…
And pray that, when this body draws no breath,
That Inner Eye will close—where'er I go.
   Though I've helped Justice prove the evil deed,
   From this "gift's" torment I shall now be freed.

XXX
Shapes of Darkness
(an Italian/Petrarchan Sonnet in Telesilleans)

The last lights off the vast West sink;
The sky darkens and shadows die.
A wan moon in the glooming sky—
The lone glimmer above Earth's brink;
Through cloud cover the stars can't wink!
Welkin's blackness can horrify;
Phantoms frighten the delving eye.
"There's movement there!" we might bethink.

"No," we say, "there is nothing there."
In stark darkness we cannot know,
Yet Fear fills in a "sight unseen."
There are things that we ought beware,
Undreamt Shapes in The Darkness grow.
Betwixt two realms they rove between!

XXXI
The Yurei

(a Japanese Sonnet—invented form
three haiku and a tanka)

departed spirits
whose reikon is tormented
can become yurei.

a death through violence—
a murder or suicide,
proper rights not done,

hatred or revenge
festering in dim spirit,
unrequited love—

these reasons could lead
to a yurei, a borei,
a sad, "ruined ghost"—
come back to dwell among us,
haunt us until they're appeased.

XXXII
Whispy Will: A Shropshire Legend
(a Rupert Brooke Sonnet)

Will the Smith's ghost's the thing that roams this marsh!
A tale all Shropshire knows. Black, evil deeds.
St. Peter sent him back—a sentence harsh—
To wander o'er the earth. His wan-light leads
Full many to their death in deep woods wet
And boggy. Best beware this boggle's light.
'Tis but a single, glowing coal, and yet
It will confound the careless caught by night.

It gives scant warmth to Will Smith's horrid form.
A phantom wraith—condemned to endless gloom—
Uses that coal to lure the living on
With *ignus fatuus*, "giddy flame." Sad harm
Will come to many, some will meet their doom,
Souls forfeit to Will-'o-the-Wisp, whose soul is gone.

Whispy Will/"Will-o-the-Wisp"

XXXIII
Fear the Wendigo
(a blank verse sonnet based upon
the rhythms of the Ojibwa and Anishinaabe
and Omushkego "Bear Spirit Song"—similar to
the same chant in several Algonquian dialects)
SEE/HEAR: https://www.youtube.com/watch?v=P8dMtCFo24o
OR: https://www.youtube.com/watch?v=3rps5yKQiSY

Fear Wendigo, Fear Wendigo. Beware, I tell you.
Cannibal beast, Cannibal beast wants to devour you!
Don't walk the deep woods; no don't dare to travel
When the cold winds come and the snow deepens
There is no safety! Not from this foul Evil,
With heart of ice and a lust for human meat.
Sunken eyeholes, fangs like daggers, gray skin stretched over
Huge bony frame. Slavering maw, bloody gore covered,
It is all Hunger—a hunger eternal!
Claws that rend flesh; two times a man's height!
Never can it be set free of its torment,
Destined to seek out the forbidden human meal.
In our North Lands, 'round the Great Lakes that should be oceans,
Roams Wendigo. Dread Wendigo. Thus, I have warned you.

XXXIV
Wendigo Chant
(an experimental sonnet with meter
loosely based upon an Ojibwe chant)

Stalking deep woodlands, seeking living prey-ay
In the bleak northern forests holding sway-ay.
Wendigo is so hungry, drooling maw-aw
Frighful canniba-al, 'gainst all Nature's law-aw.
You will know it is close by-iy, rotten
Stench on deathly cold bree-eeze; grim
Bloody ground and the scattered gnawed-through bo-ones,
Prove the terrible truth, the Tale not forgot-ten,
Wendigo's ah-are real, and you've found him!
Shun, you travelers, frozen forest zo-ones,
For the Wendigo roams the wintry ni-ight.
Twice as tall as a man, with gray, taunt ski-in,
Gruesome, blood-oozing lips, self-gnawed, whi-ite
Fangs show, yearning for human taste—a great si-in.

Fear the Wendigo

XXXV
Cycles
(a Quatrain-Couplet Blend Sonnet—invented form)

They do not know; they cannot feel my curse.
Of course, I do my best to conceal the pain.
I've suffered many years—But now it's worse,
each time more intense. Back when it first began,
it was only the Dread that grew until release.
Then, back to Dread—slight Hope that it might cease.
How many have I slain? Lost long ago
the count I sought to keep. But now I know
there is no use keeping tally of my sins.
Each Blood Night passes….Then it again begins!
The months plod on, Old Time moves on apace.
The agony mounts; there never is a lull.
My next victims won't live to describe my face.
Ah! Finally come round…
the moon is at the full.

XXXVI
On Samhain Winds
(a English/Shakespearean Sonnet in the Irish
meter of Dechnad Mor)

On Samhain* winds we hear whispers;
Wights have hither wandered.
Gone even echoes of vespers—
vain hope that unsundered
will be *Veil 'Twixt Realms*—untattered
'til the sun's next setting.
Not so! *Wall Between Worlds* shattered,
split, sundered! Thus letting
in ghosts, grim ghouls, foulest Evils:
weird were-things, vile vampires,
fearsome fiends, fell phantoms, devils
of dire *Dark*. What transpires
As this long, strange night is passing—
The sum of terrors amassing.

*The Irish Gaelic pronunciation of "Samhain" is *Sa-Wen*.

XXXVII
A Druid's Divinations
(an Ae Freslige Sonnet—invented form)

The wet wood is glistening,
in the weird wan light shining—
Man in the Moon listening
to the druid's divining
by Sacred Oak, uttering
spells to invoke deep answers.

Winged things of night fluttering
'round ring of frenzied dancers;
wheeling birds, bats chattering.

The pagan priest's voice rises…
din of forest shattering
to silent awe; reprises
the ancient rites done under
this Oak, this Moon of Wonder.

XXXVIII
We Ghouls

(a sonnet in the Welsh form of the Rhupunt)

We are the Ghouls, and grisly pools form when we drool each time we dine.
Those reft of breath who've met their death, gone underneath—their taste is fine!
When corpses fall into Our Hall, we gather all that we can find.
From times of old our story's told: we, when you're cold, feed on your kind.
We rob the grave so we can savor putrid flavor in fanged maw.
Sweet to us—War provides great gore as we explore each field of fray;
We, with great guile, your dead defile through black night while your folk *YOU* slay.
Hunger increased, on Death we feast—the Primal Beast is but our Law.
We prefer graveyards, but no slaves to that behavior or such zone.
If—chance you pace through forlorn place—you'll find our trace. You're not alone!
We can shift shape! Our mouths agape, there's no escape—we'll drink your blood.
And a young child, so tender, mild. Don't be beguiled…we love such food.
You hold Life dear. But let's be clear. When we are near, we just may kill!
We prefer rot! But—if you're caught, though "New Death's" hot—the heart is still.

XXXIX
The Corpse Bird
[Aderyn y Corph]

(a Couplet Sonnet in the Welsh meter of Cyhydedd Naw Ban,
making use of the harmonies of Cynghanedd Sain
and Cynghanedd Lusg—a Cyhydedd Naw Ban Sonnet—invented form)

There is a dreaded bird of legends
Whose dire call impending death portends.
Whene're the *Aderyn y Corph* is heard,
And *"dewch!"*—"Come ye hither!" is the word,
You must prepare for end to breathing
For all about foul Death is wreathing
His ring to fling you into his fold;   *sain*
Then you're old as you'll ever be old.

This dread Thing has nor feathers nor wings,
And some say, after its Death-Call sings,
To Earth's End it goes—and then wends past!   *lusg*
To a different plane of being, vast,
Unknowable to our mortal minds—
Where Reason dies, Sanity unwinds!

Aderyn y Corph

XL
The Hag of the Mist
(*Grwrach y Rhibyn*[1])
[an "Envelope Sonnet "done in the Welsh meter of Rhupunt]

An awful tryst—Hag of the Mist you chance to meet.
On leather wings, this Terror brings portent of doom.
On foggy night, this awful wight through mists may loom:
Ghastly of face, her form debased, in her you greet
Your likely death. Bereft of breath, your days are done!
And if you hear, as she draws near, Cyhyraeth's[2] call—
Her ghostly moan—you well may groan before you fall.
Hearing that voice, you have no choice. Of Hope there's none.

Mere skin and bone, near skeleton when she appears.
Sometimes mere wraith, she's—by my Faith!—invisible
No form at all, but just a call—you'll hear it thrice;
Each cry more faint. And there's no Saint, to quell your fears.
Your kin will grieve. Do not believe She's mythical.
Come day or night, know well the plight. Your Life's the price.

NOTES:
[1] The *Grwrach y Rhibyn* [grow-rock a ribban] or "Hag of the Mist" is a
monstrous Welsh spirit in the shape of a hideously ugly woman, harpy-like in appearance, hair unkempt, wizened and withered with leathery
wings, long, black teeth, and pale, corpse-like features. A harbinger of
Death.

[2] This spirit is often conflated with the *Cyhyraeth* [ka-har-eth] or "skeleton,
mere thing of skin and bone"—but often more incorporeal and a disembodied doleful voice calling out before a death.

XLI
Crossing Over:
A Nekuia in Five Sonnets

I found a way to pay—two coins of gold
placed on my eyelids bound with folds of black
tied tight around my head. The Boatman told
me, "None alive have crossed and then come back."
     "But what about famed Orpheus seeking Euridice,
or Theseus trying to save Persphone,
or wily Odysseus who was allowed to pass
in search of wisdom from the dead Tieresias
and spoke with Achilles—who'd 'rather be a slave
than king among the breathless, gibbering dead'?"
     "Do you think yourself an equal to those men,
the greatest of a Great Age? Do you believe you have
the Power to thwart that Night, this Land of Dread?
I'll wait here for a while. But I must go back again.

     "The dead mount quickly. In droves they come. No end
to my weariness. They will not cease to wend
toward Acheron—and I their Ferryman, Guide
across this River to this Nether side,
I, Charon, I too must do my part.
The Three Fates have decreed it from the start.
     "Go now and see the woeful, wailing shades,
those dwellers in the dark Demesne of Hades.
Know that if I am gone—should you return—
that you are forever here. Too late to yearn
for the Land of the Living—though you can see its shore
just over yonder. That zone you'll see no more."
     And so, I turned and crossed that beach's sand,
blacker than night—and into the Foredoomed Land.

I found the cave mouth guarded by the Dog,
He whose three necks each held a snarling head.
I had no lyre to lull it into sleep
like Orpheus. But my spell cast The Fog
of Somnus—learned from forbidden text I'd read.
Quite soon I was able to pass the Hound, to creep
up to the gate, above which hung a sign:

"Abandon Hope, all ye who enter here."
I entered and walked down a steep incline.
    There is a cold wind ever wafting there.
Mid darkest shadows, shades' moaning never ceases,
but shifts in abhorrent chorus—awful to hear!—
bewailing their plight, the Fate from which no release is.
The Dead flocked 'round. But none dared to come near.

I had prepared all—before I crossed Styx flood,
I poured into a pan a skin of blood!
No wine would summon the shade I sought to find,
she who had been these five weeks in my mind
and in my heart. My cherished wife had died
too suddenly, too soon. I'd not be denied!
I'd studied all dark, occult, forbidden lore;
I'd bring her back with me—to Live once more!
    She came. She was in awe to see me there.
With spells, I'd caught Old Hades unaware.
Yes, like brave Orpheus—but I would not fail!
We'd not look back…no Triple-Dog blocked our trail.
I noticed that Persephone was crying?
Charon, amazed, completed my wife's undying.

    He ferried us back. Now she is here with me.
But we have nothing of the bliss now past.
There is a dead look in her demon eye.
This Thing is not my wife! It is not she!
    Yes, the Living can go, return—but at the last—
The Dead should remain. And now I yearn to die.
Alas! I've sought these months to send her back,
More of forbidden scrolls—no lines unlearned.
Attempts to unmake her—there has been no lack.
    I'd as soon in fiery Phlegethon be burned,
Or that I might, drowned in Styx, forget this sin.
But no. I shall arrange to go back again.
No coins, no blindfold. I'll see once more my friend—
Who'll ferry me across.…This time my rightful end

XLII
El Roba Chicos
[The Child Snatcher)]
(a Double Seguidilla Sonnet—invented form)

In Mexico children fear
El Roba Chicos
Who snatches up bad children
Into his bag, then goes
Back to his lair to eat them.
They are warned. They know
Misbehaving might mean Death!

El Viejo del Saco,
"Old Man with the Bag,"
In Chile, Argentina—
If you have been bad—
The same ending may result:
Misbehave—you have
Invited a grim visit.

XLIII
Spectral Zones

(a Rondel Supreme Sonnet—invented form)

There be weird spectral zones well-hidden,
Yet there be some who choose to go.
Of arcane wisdom they would know—
The eldritch spells that are forbidden!

These I have sought, although long chidden
By foes and fellow alchemists enow.
There be weird spectral zones well-hidden,
Yet I was one who chose to go.

And now my nights are horror-ridden,
My conjurings a source of endless woe!
Bones of the damned—dead long ago!
I once dared pass that human middan.
There be weird spectral zones forbidden.
Alas! I was one who dared to go.

XLIV
Plenilune
(a Bowlesian/Australian Sonnet)

The nights swing round again toward plenilune.
There is no casting off this curse I bear.
My howls, inhuman, soon will tear the air
As I go hunting 'neath that dooming moon,
How many months this now-accustomed plight
Has been my wretched woe to re-enact?
How many innocents have I attacked
And slain beneath the sable shield of night?
Perhaps next time my soul will find release?
Some bullet, blade, bludgeon of silver made
Might find my body—Yes! for this I've prayed!
Until Death comes, I know I'll have no peace.
And yet, tomorrow's moon's at perigee
And at the full! And hunger grows in me.

XLV
The Find

*"Ms Roberta Chambers, formerly of Salem, has
purchased the home at 319 Ashton Street, Arkham,
from the estate of Miss Agnes Clark-Smith.
    The house has been vacant since the owner's
disappearance in 1952 and in need of significant
repairs, but Ms Chambers plans to begin renovation
as soon as she settles in....*
    —*The Arkham Chronicle*
    Society Column, 9 May 1975

She'd lived in the old house only two weeks before
She sensed that something about the place was wrong.
She thought, "Perhaps why I got it for a song?"
An odd, low sound that she could not ignore...
Something sliding across the attic floor
And just above her bed. A low, grating sound.
At any rate, *What Something?* had to be found,
So, she lowered the trap-door ladder to explore.

Midst the clutter, she saw the trunk, in the lamp's dim light
And the dustless track left behind where it had slid
A full dozen feet. But she neared—despite growing dread.

She opened it...screamed...a shriek far beyond simple fright
When she saw what within that chest of horror was hid.
The mummified corpse of a woman...but missing the head.

XLVI
Object of His Desire

He'd found the thing in a strange, old antique shop
On a dismal by-street in the ancient town.
Hideous in all aspects…but he could not stop
From wanting it. He could not put it down!
He asked the man who owned the place, "How much?"
The fish-faced fellow answered, "Not for sale."
"I'll pay you any price," his lust was such
For the statue—And so begins my tale.
At last, a deal was struck. He had his prize.
He paid no attention to the evil grin
Upon the old man's face as he left. His eyes
Were on *The Thing*. It's shape was not akin
To any living creature that he knew.
The idol effused…Reality *askew!*

Likely that's why he wanted the eldritch shape,
Carved of some weird and unknown hard, green stone.
From its allure he would find no escape.
The monstrous thing sat on a carven throne:
Its head cephalopod with tentacles around;
Its body lionesque, but spreading wings like a bat
Flared from its back. But the expression found
On its face, beyond all trace of doubt was that
Of pure malevolence. Its horrid, hideous form
Was made more awful by that visage grim—
Yet he still cherished it e'en through the storm
Of ridicule. Friends soon abandoned him.
Acquaintances and family thought him mad
In fact—to idolize the weird idol that he had.

"Get rid of that Evil. Toss it in the sea!"
His priest had said. "That thing is blasphemy
In stone! My Son, you must be rid
Of this foul object that any god would forbid!"
But his obsession with it did not wane.
It went with him, wherever he would go,
Tucked in his coat. Soon he could not refrain
From talking of it. "Everyone must know
It's power, the wonder of its message clear!
Just listen! Only listen—you will hear!"
His health, as many noted, soon declined.
Within the month, he'd clearly lost his mind.
They found him clutching the idol in his hand,
Half-eaten by crabs, face-down on the dark sea strand.

XLVII
Reflection

(a Sicilian Sonnet)

At first she thought, "An optical illusion."
Her image in the mirror seemed…"not quite right."
Disturbing apprehension and confusion
Began to grow…but soon it turned to fright.
 For Reason offered no valid conclusion
Why her image seemed to show a different wight!
Its movements lagged or varied. An intrusion
Upon her sanity must be her plight!

But, gradually, very slowly, her relief
Came when the synchronized projection
Of movement had returned. But it was brief—
This respite from all Logic's Laws rejection—
At last, she saw! Beyond all disbelief,
In horror, she knew—now She was the reflection!

XLVIII
A Phantom Whisper
(A sonnet in the form of the Spanish
Cuaderna Via [the "four-fold way"])

"I know not why I answered my old friend's most strange request,
To meet him at that Hell Gate, that castle beyond the West
That very few may access. Yet, at his urgent behest,
I made my long way thither on that most ill-fated quest.

"Those ruins of stone are damned, accursed in our ancient lore,
Home to myriad Evils, where past The Forbidden Door
Dwell beings from "the Outside," a place of abject Horror
Most think are only legends—impossible myths of yore.

"The sun was dying, blood-red, on the last day of the year,
Behind those fierce fangs of stone as I drew near and nearer.
My fellow mage then met me. 'It will take us both, I fear,
To hold against The Darkness that will all too soon appear.'

"Yes, we stood there united. But our warding spells were vain.
We now are ghosts on the wind—and They have come forth again!"

XLIX
Contrarium Visum
[a *Vue Opposée*]
(a French Sonnet)

"….So sad the field, so waste the ground,
So curst with an old despair,….
So lonely, too, so more than sad,…
I wondered what more could Nature add
To the sum of its miseries…
And then—I saw the trees.

"Skeletons gaunt that gnarled the place,
Twisted and torn they rose--
The tortured bones of a perished race
Of monsters no mortal knows,
They startled the mind's repose.

"And a man stood there, as still as moss,
A lichen form that stared;
With an old blind hound that, at a loss,
Forever around him fared
With a snarling fang half bared.

"I looked at the man; I saw him plain;
Like a dead weed, gray and wan,
Or a breath of dust. I looked again--
And man and dog were gone,
Like wisps of the graying dawn…."

—Madison Cawein, from "The Waste Land"*
January 1913 issue of *Poetry*

"Ah, yes, my faithful Blue, I see you've nosed him out.
A new "Live One" has somehow found our spectral wood.
Though blind, your second sight would lead you to this food.
But let us merely show ourselves—he'll turn about.
It's strange how many find our wood. But there's no doubt
That many wanderers, through sad, cursed lives have stood
Past this vast gulf—a seeming field! Cross if they could!"
"He sees us! Dim, weird shapes will stop him, change his route.

"Now, like wisps of the graying dawn—we disappear!
He turns, hastens back through the mist, heart full of fear."

Such are many contacts when dead and living meet.
Other, Parallel Worlds, most living refuse to ken.
Some seek to summon hither—or would cross! Retreat
Is best when borders fall 'twixt Now, and Then, and When.

*[Note: Cawein's "The Waste Land" is considered by many to be one
of the chief inspirations of Eliot's poem.]

L
Skinner
(a "melded" sonnet sequence in Pararhyme)

They'd found the man entirely stripped of flesh,
"Flayed while he was still alive," the coroner said.
"I can't imagine how intense the pain," he sighed,
But then proceeded with this work. The flash
That leapt from the scalpel's shining blade
In the room's stark light made Agent Hopkins blink.
He was not at all surprised by the lack of blood.
"Complete exsanguination!" The coroner's face turned blank.
But Hopkins had expected that. He knew "his man,"
At least his man's MO, but he knew no name,
No face to look for. But it had been "the right moon"—
Just at first quarter. Again, the sense of numb
Futility set in. He'd tracked this fiend
Across the country with nary a clue to find.
The FBI had formed the select team,
And Hopkins had been named SAIC—
He knew he'd likely earned it over time:
Skilled profiler? Successful cases? Who could say?
But this devil was different—killed the agent's old belief:
"No matter how bad, there's some good in everyone."
And Hopkins knew, deep down, that—if and when
He found this fiend—he would not let him live.
This latest victim made the total ten!
From Maine here to Missouri, a child, a teen,
Six in their 20s to 40s, two old men,
Both males and females—what could all that mean?
There was no doubt about the horrid Way
He killed. But who could guess the Why?
Much less the How? The bodies all were skinned,
Drained of all blood, the neck wounds had been scanned,
Examined closely for weapon marks or type.
Nothing was found to match the depth or size
Of those grim gouges. Hopkins sought to seize
On just what that quarter moon meant. Any tip
Would have been welcome. He was stumped.
The only other pattern was the East to West

Trail of the crimes. All other leads proved a waste
Of time. Dead ends. Only the ghastly MO, stamped
On each scene of slaughter. The only other note
Of import was the fairly regular distances between
The murders—170 miles, give or take. No, not
Exact, but interestingly close.
                                        And when
Word came from Central Kansas of a survivor!
Hopkins and Agent Smith jumped in their car.

• • •

The man was still in shock, the Intensive Care
Doctor proclaimed, "This was some carnivore,
Some animal—I don't know what—but nothing human
Could make these wounds! On what skin remains
On the arms, torso, and on this poor man's
Legs—claw marks spaced too wide for any man
To make.
            "How is it that he was found alive?"
Asked Hopkins.
                    "Two fellows out hunting, I believe,"
The doctor answered, "came upon whatever beast
Was savaging this fellow. They shot at it. It fled,
They said, into the trees. I've done the best
That I can do," he added. But half his skin is flayed!
    "There's no hope, I'm afraid. He's heavily sedated,
And I think we must induce a coma soon.
Could this poor fellow's fate somehow be tied
To all those serial murders that I've seen
In the news of late?"
                        "I'm afraid I can't
Comment on that, doctor, but I must count
On you to keep the details of this quiet
For now, while we investigate. But the men
Who chased 'whatever' off—where are they at?"
    "I'm pretty sure they're with the local police.
They were treated here too for shock, but unless

57

They've been released from questioning,
The cops took them in to grill them on "The Thing."'
Then Hopkin's said, "We have no time to lose!"

. . .

    The hunters were still being asked just what they knew
By the local police. But Hopkins broke in, "Now,
I know this will be a repeat, but what did you see?"
    "Well, Sir, I can't rightly say just what we saw.
It warn't no human, I can tell you that!
It was just before dawn. When we saw the Thing I thought,
'It's a black bear at a kill'—we have a few, you know…"
    "I thought that too," the other said, "but that
Was no bear, nor what it fed on a deer! I knew
When it turned toward us. I swear the Thing was green!
Dark green, and scaled like a fish! We heard a groan
From whatever that manfish was feeding on."
    "That's right!" the other agreed. We both shot
At the thing. It ran."
                        Still white as a sheet,
Both men asserted that their tale was true.
The local cops scoffed. But Hopkins just said, "Try
To point out the exact place on this map. Where
Did this happen? It's damned important that we're
There as soon as possible, to track it down,
To catch or kill it—that's what must be done!"
    "That explains it all. The killer is not a man," thought
Hopkins, "but some weird, unholy Thing that
Has some need in such a way to hunt
And kill!" Just what it was there was no hint.
    "It happened in the woods just south of Hays,
Not far from Big Creek, but that damned thing has
Me spooked. I'm not going out there again,"
Said one, "If you go best take a damn big gun."
"The spot is here," the other said. "And I'll not
Go with you either. It skinned that man as neat
As one can skin a rabbit! And the skin it ate!
Or seemed so. Weren't a piece of skin left at
The place we scared it off and found that man
Or what was left of him. What can it mean?"

• • •

"What can it mean, indeed," was Hopkins thought,
On the way out to the map-marked place that
Had been the sight of the attack. He only knew
That this trail of horror had to end—end now!
He loaded slugs and double-O buckshot
Into the riot gun with 12-guage bore
"If I find this Thing, this thing that is 'no bear,'
I'll kill this beast! This evil, bastard shit!"

• • •

He and Smith and eight other men beside
Spread out into the forest from the road.
"Keep your head on a swivel," Hopkins said,
We have to find this creature and be well rid
Of it."
      "Despite their yarn I still think the killer
Must be a man—perhaps in some disguise?
We simply have to drive him from his lair."
Just then some fleeting movements met their gaze.
"I think we've got him," Smith then shouted out.
  "I hope you're right," said Hopkins. "'Him not 'IT.'"
Then all the men walked on without a word,
All sensing they were hunting something weird.
And just then—there peered out through the trees—
A being that all sanity betrays!

As the hunter said, the thing was scaled and green,
Hunched over, but bipedal, bigger than any man.
Its slavering maw seemed set in a weird, grim grin.
Hopkins and Smith and two of the sheriff's men
Began at once to shoot. The Thing cried out.
It ran, then stumbled toward them, through the fire
And hail of lead. And much to their surprise
The Thing kept coming! There seemed no stopping it.

It lurched ahead, seeming to sense their fear,
But then it fell…yet—once again—it rose,
Straight toward Hopkins! Ten feet away it fell
For the last time. The men cheered to see it fall.

Hopkins fired twice more into the crumpled heap,
Tossed down the shotgun, drew his pistol from his hip
And fired all fifteen rounds into the beast.

It took another minute for him to dare
To walk up to examine this creature dire
And horrible to look at.
                              "A man somehow debased?"
He wondered to himself. "No, no way it's a man.
A thing from outer space? What can this mean?
Some science meddling gone horribly amiss?
He grew ill as he viewed the gory mass—
To see the terrible razor tooth that it
Used to flay off the flesh that it would eat!
And the horrid siphon tooth—a hollow dagger blade
It used to draw out all its victim's blood!

                              ...

He barely had time to turn in terror when
Smith screamed out, "*Oh God! There's more than one!*"

LI
The Mad Seer Has a Vision
(a sonnet in Lesser Asclepiads*)

"In the West the fierce moon hangs as a blood-red sphere
On the edge of the world. Perched before final fall
Into blackness. A Night, stark as oblivion,
On the Solstice of June—just at the midnight hour—
Has begun. Soon the vast, eldritch, and cosmic depths
Of the sky hang above, lowering gloomily
Over Earth, a forlorn orb in that infinite sea.

Soon abroad o'er the land Creatures of Darkness creep.
'Neath the ocean's ink depths, there where he dreamt and slept,
Ancient Cthulhu awakes! Eons have rolled o'er him.
Though in Death, in a Dream, Now is his time come round,
And the skies and the sea open to let *Them* in
Or come forth from their lairs, hidden for long epochs:
The Old Ones have returned!" This is my vision clear.

LII
Stone Memory
(a 6-2-6 Sonnet —invented form)

"It's like a tape recording," Aimes explained.
"Some trauma or some horrid deed is captured
Within material things!—even in the surrounding air!—
As Lethbridge held. Something is kept, contained
Around the very site. Where later, all enraptured,
The visitor sees a 'replay'—but nothing's there…
Really. They are not actual 'ghosts' per se
But merely 'images' performing in a 'play'
As it were. There is no chance of physical harm."
　So saying, he led us on into the dark
And sinuous corridors of Castle Doom.
Yet I wondered why he clutched an onyx charm.

That evil play began.… Then from the blackness—Hark!
Aimes was dead wrong! We fled from that cursed tomb.

LIII
Wages of Sin

(an Englyn Byr Cwca Sonnet,—invented form)

He delved into arcane tomes—
Not only secret but cursed, forbidden!
To ken what Darkness roams
This side of the veil—hidden
Within those stained, damned, moldering pages,
Ages lost…Then, bidden
By words of Evil Sages,
He used the awful knowledge he had won!
Soon undone, the wages
For conjurings he had done
Must needs be paid. "Devil will have his due."
Full soon he knew that none
Of his precautions worked. There came in view
A *Thing* to claim his soul. This too he knew.

LIV
Enlightenment

They brought me to this place. I don't know why.
It seems a hospital with many rooms,
But, horribly, about its corridors fly
What must be ghosts! Free of their dismal tombs.
And there are doctors here—and orderlies…
Large men dressed all in white and frightening.
A madhouse then! And patients such as these—
Clearly insane! Each night my fright is heightening.
The inmates scream and gibber. Do they see
These *Others* with us in this Bedlam too—
These many phantoms roaming ceaselessly?
Am I insane? Remember!…Could it be true?!
  I am a member here of two sad hosts:
  Mad killer!—now dead—belonging with these ghosts.

LV
Eidolon Tetratych
[After Thomas Bailey Aldrich's, "Eidolon"—
The four epigraphs are sections of that sonnet.]

I. The Night's Children
Those forms we fancy shadows, those strange lights
That flash on lone morasses, the quick wind
That smites us by the roadside are the Night's
Innumerable children.

Near-hidden in the depths of Night—but darker—
Are the myriad beings from a different Zone.
Those uneasy times you feel you are not alone…
You are right! Those phantom dim marsh lights grow starker
And flash in brutal brilliance if you fare too close
The sudden frosty breeze that chills your cheek,
Might well be Something one should never seek.
Night's Spawn—those shadowy forms know no repose.

Of the vast and countless legion of the ancient dead
A still vast portion linger near our plain.
A huge, horrific number who remain
With powers to journey back and hither tread.
Oh yes! They are with us here, our plague and plight.
They are the spectral Children of the Night.

II. Unconfined
…Unconfined
By shroud or coffin, disembodied souls,
Still on probation, steal into the air
From ancient battlefields and churchyard knolls
At the day's ending…

As day and life depart and the lych bell tolls,
And corpse remains, the spirit gone, that knell
Most often means departure for those souls
To wend their ways to Heaven or to Hell.
But there are many—far too many—wights
Who are condemned to linger near us here.

Though many are merely lost, Some are to Fear!
And can return to us to haunt our nights.

A soldier slain in a battle long forgotten,
Who himself relished slaying other men.
And others who believed it no great sin
To use their fellows ill—such souls are rotten!
The misbegotten, most amoral brood
Whose thoughts were foul and deeds were never good.

III. The Dusk of Hope
…Pestilence and despair
Fly with the startled bats at set of sun;

No, They are not confined in crypt or coffin
These bringers of stark Fear and dire Despair.
Foreboded by foul, pestilential air
When they impinge upon us here—quite often
Miasmatic mistsm the horrid dim-lit *Portal*
Demark their entry points. You must beware
Their presence—sensed first in the very air!
Sickening, chill, the bane of all who are mortal.

They are the ones for whom all hope has fled,
The foredoomed spirits of the restless dead.
Among fleet flying bats at set of sun
They hover close—and closer 'til the dawn
But the Night is far their favorite demesne.
Then they roam free. And woe if they are seen!

66

Especially cursed are those who most foully slew
Their fellow creatures by cruel plot or plan:
Whether an assassin of a king or queen,
Or some foul fiend, killing one they never knew
To satisfy a lust for pain and blood,
Or take a life seeking to gain in power.
Their essence is ever condemned to loom and lower—
A curse upon us, *Antithesis of Good.*

The great inheritance of a soul that might have been
Has been sold or thrown aside by these Long Lost.
These and their ilk come back through that Door, once crossed
Was never meant to be journeyed through again.
And so, we must know, who dwell on the Living Side,
Night's Children return through a Portal open wide.

LVI
When the moon is full, large looming
(a Korean Kasa Sonnet—invented form)

When the moon is full, large looming,
Then the werefolk stalk hapless prey.
Nights are more dread at plenilune,
Frights more frequent 'neath that round face.
  Curse of a bite survived is theirs—
Worse than the death they might have had.
  Seeming elsetimes—"normal people,"
Gleaming fangs show from fear-furred face,
Features contort—lycanthropoid
Creatures will prowl the wan-lit night.
  Strange shapes lope, half-wolf, half-human,
Range through woodlands, over the moors,
  Heed this caution, for these grim beasts
Feed on the ghastly meal of Man.

LVII
Spring-Heeled Jack
(a Pie Quebrado Sonnet—invented form)

Rooftop to rooftop he can leap,
Darker by far than night sky deep,
In cloak of black.
Clawed hands and eyes of fiery red,
He breathes blue flame—a Thing to dread!
It's Spring-Heeled Jack!

Some say his claws are knives of steel;
Some, "He's a myth. He can't be real."
But victim's say
His visage is a horror stark,
Devil-horned helm. Evil most Dark,
He shuns the day.

In every British shire they tell
Young children, "Fear this fiend from Hell."

LVIII
Now Is the Bright Nighttime
(a "Curtal" English Sonnet—invented form)

Now is the bright nighttime of plenilune.
Through the chill air, a drawn-out howl is heard.
A monstrous thing stalks under that round moon.

 Most times—a man—but now a creature furred
And fanged and clawed:—a Lycanthrope!—
A fiend compelled, by bestial hunger spurred.

Not manlike, but with wolven leap and lope,
He moves through woodlands, over open plain.
For any human met—there is no hope.

Come morning, he, so foully cursed, would fain—
Be just a man again.

LIX
Nocte Viatores

There are weird ones who only move by night,
Travelling solely by light of moon and star,
Cursing the Day and shunning its stark light.
Faring from Deeps of Dark beyond the far-
Flung galaxies, black holes, and nebulae,
From cosmic depths of unimagined void,
Beyond what our strongest telescopes can see.
Their mission: that our known world be destroyed!
The Old Ones and their Spawn. Fell eldritch tales
Relate their expulsion—Oh! So long ago!
But They return! And strict, cold Reason fails
To encompass what no living soul should know.
More horrible! These awful Wanderers in the dark—
Not mere Minions…for their Masters soon embark!

LX
Strange Blooms
[from the journal of Dr. Randall Derwent,
discovered at the abandoned campsite
of four botanical researchers]

I. Day One: Getting Near the Site

"We've traveled far into the Honduran hills,
Following reports of new-found marvelous blooms
Deep in those jungles dark. Even at noon the glooms
Oppressed my spirit, gave me shuddering chills
Despite the sweltering heat. And fauna noise that fills
"The Bush"— cacophony that shouts that danger looms
Far "spookier" than the silence of cold tombs.

But we seek the type of discovery that thrills
The botanist's heart. The tales seemed fantasy:
Towering stalks, surmounted by red flowers,
Growing from double roots and sprouting limbs.
If true, it will be a great discovery!

. . .

We've made a base camp, but the fleeting hours
Of day have caught us and a stormy welkin dims."

II. Day Two: The Discovery

"Our camp is just a mile below the site
And we set out an hour after the dawn,
Following a tremendous, thunderous stormy night
And, strangely, the animal noises all had gone?
Amazingly, those wild, weird tales are true!
We reached an open space where—much amazed!—
Far more than just a few strange flowers grew—
If one can call those "flowers" on which we gazed.
The tales are true! Some grew from double stalks,
With two "limbs" sprouting out on either side,
But most arose from four stems, had no "limbs?"
They covered the ground across that clearing wide.

We began at once more closely to explore
The region around that glade where animal life
Was strangely quite—though the day before was rife
With cries of animals and birds. The night's downpour
We thought must have brought that stillness strange.
The red blooms we found must propagate by spore
Rather than seed—for, while we searched the glade,
Those crimson blossoms spewed out puffs of dust,
In spouts of rusty-hewed foul-smelling must...."

III. Day Three: Thoughts on the New Species

"Those spores were choking, and they burnt our eyes.
Johnson and Smythe were both in extreme pain.
The way those plants work I can but surmise,
But now— next morning—I cannot explain!
Smythe, Johnson, Ivanov—all are gone!
And those weird plants are growing in our camp!
The day is not as hot; it's just past dawn,
Yet I am sweating hard. A miasmic damp
Is all about this place. Trying to move,
My arms are sluggish—my legs can only lift
Me to standing! The sun looks strange above,
And all about those damned spores are adrift!
I'm frightened! What can this dull feeling mean?
Oh, God! My skin! My skin is turning green..."

LXI
Malum ex Machina
(an irregular sonnet and a Scupham Sonnet)

1

As far as paranormal science went,
He was the foremost theorist in the land.
From early days in college he had spent
Now forty years, seeking to understand
Those things that lie beyond most human ken:
Clairvoyance, telekinesis, remote viewing,
Spirits from Beyond—demonic and ghostly—
Satanic rites, ectoplasm, Shadow Men....

Of late, his interest in EVPs renewing,
He'd improved upon the proven devices—mostly
Derived from original "tech" but clearer,
With more immediate feedback of "The Voice."
It seemed to draw the phenomenon's source nearer
And also force that closeness with no choice!

2

Indeed, it seemed the thing could actually summon
Entities from that other realm than ours.
And more, much more than single words and phrases,
Full, clearly spoken sentences were common,
And he began to wonder just what powers
The apparatus held. He worked in phases:

First he would merely document conversations
He'd held with Them. He kept a neat notebook.
Next, keen curiosity made him query
About their region. And he felt elation
When next they, through video channels, let him look!
Though their words thrilled, those visions made him wary!

Too late he realized he'd created a portal
For Horrors—both terrible—and immortal!

LXII
Not That Room!
(from the diary of Ambrose Algernon Gilman—final entry)

"The mansion has come down at last to me.
God knows I've waited long enough to earn
My birthright. Father lived to ninety-three
And would not cede it sooner. May he burn!"

"The place is mine now, and I'll see what's hidden
In that locked room, behind the thick oak door.
Both grandfather and he'd warned, '*It's forbidden,
That's all you need to know.*' They said no more.

"I'll not be kept from something of great worth
Because of some taboo, some senseless curse.
I have the keys. What's there is mine by birth…"

The truth behind the taboo was much worse.
What little remained of him would leave no doubt
How awful was the horror he'd let out.

LXIII
Carcosa Twilight
(a Kashmiri Vakh Sonnet-—an invented form)

Twin suns set behind the lake.
Cloud waves break along the shore.
Strange moons sail in somber skies.
Carcosa beckons!—as of yore.

Black stars rise in welkin weird.
Shadows grow, umbrageous dark.
Shapes are moving—to be feared!
Suddenly a wailing! Hark!

From the Hyades, a song
Fast enthralls the foredoomed throng,
Yellow tatters of the King
Flap in foetid wind. They sing
Of the loss of Lives and Souls,
As Carcosa's Black Bell tolls.

LXIV
Reflection
(a Sicilian Sonnet)

At first she thought, "An optical illusion."
Her image in the mirror seemed…"not quite right."
Disturbing apprehension and confusion
Began to grow…but soon it turned to fright.
 For Reason offered no valid conclusion
Why her image seemed to show a different wight!
Its movements lagged or varied. An intrusion
Upon her sanity must be her plight!

But, gradually, very slowly, her relief
Came when the synchronized projection
Of movement had returned. But it was brief—
This respite from all Logic's Laws rejection—
At last, she saw! Beyond all disbelief,
In horror, she knew—now She was the reflection!

LXV
We Only Know a Name
(Quatrain-Couplet Blend Sonnet—invented form)

Time has flown since a century-and-a-half ago
A heinous killer prowled East London's paths;
A villain whose name we'll likely never know
Left in his wake horrific aftermaths:
Multiple murders, mutilations grim,
Disfigurements, disembowelings dire—
Yet he was never caught! No proof of him
Who, no doubt now, burns in Hell's hottest fire.
Working for one more gin or one night's doss,
Enduring shame for a tiny pittance earned,
Not knowing just how great would be their loss,
Their suffering, their final lesson learned:
Tabrum? perhaps, then Nichols, Chapman, Stride
All walked the East End streets—and there they died.

The last—it seems? Mary Kelly lost her life
In Miller's Court, cruelly carved by this monster's knife.
Unfortunately, police work in those times,
Was woefully unprepared to solve these crimes.
Oh, there were suspects—many!—were and are,
But no investigation has gone very far.
A cryptic message in chalk quick washed away,
A package with gory kidney wrapped within;
Suspects abound, yet—elusive to this day—
Just who was guilty of this trail of sin.
But a letter, likely fake, writ in blood red
(Of its lack of provenance most are quite sure),
It's rambling message generally unknown—Instead
It is well-remembered for its signature:

"I want to get to work right away…good luck.
Yours Truly Jack the Ripper." That has stuck.

LXVI
Veniat ei Malum qui Vocat Malum
[Let evil come to him who calls evil.]

The grimoire held such secrets that he craved.
That dark book writ in blood and grimly cloaked
In human skin. Yet he was so depraved
He cared not what his chantings had provoked.
The words leapt from the pages as he scanned
With rowan wand, thinking it would protect
Him from whatever wights this book—long banned—
Were summoned forth. But that desired effect
Of safety—despite the invocation of Hell—
Was hopeless, and his trust had been in vain…
For *The Thing* that answered his well-spoken spell
Brought such stark horror and such surfeit of pain
That his mind dissolved before his body burned.
The wages of the summoner were earned.

LXVII
Cacachromy

1
That day, he woke to something very strange.
Just after wiping "sleep" from waking eyes,
He was amazed to find the very range
Of colors of his world was wrong. His surprise
Became complete bewilderment. "There must
Be something wrong." Then, "This can't be right!"
"Perhaps by light of day they will adjust?"
He went outside. But worse—the day was night!
The sky was dark, the "colors"—negative
Images of remembered normalcy!

The optometrist couldn't help. "I cannot give
An explanation. No defect I can see.
My best advice, if this complaint persists,
Find if some brain anomaly exists."

2
Neurology could find no pathology,
No physical abnormality could be seen.
The dawns stayed dark. The gloamings bright. And he
Saw green things "glow," human skin tones sickly green!

A friend, whose hobby was photography,
Projected color negatives on one wall.
These looked to him as his lost reality,
Gave his new world more reason to appall.

"It's not my eyes or brain—it's in my mind!"
He had to conclude. "I must be going mad!"
But no psychiatrist he found could find
An explanation for this curse he had.
  And worse, to his greatly horrified surprise,
  He now saw the "colors" when he closed his eyes!

3
The waking memory of those awful hues
Remained somehow with eyes shut! And his dreams
Were nightmared. Soon, he started to confuse
Sleep and waking life. Were his wild screams
Subconscious somnolent cries—or were they real?
Now, not only Space but Time was rearranged.

One final shift in his vision would reveal
That more than his eyesight and mind had changed.
There were more horrors now: monstrously weird "creatures,"
Beings even a sick soul could not draw.
And their "colors" that should not be —worse than their features—
Defied what he knew of every Natural Law.

He had no choice. So, that same daylit night,
He ended his life, his mind, his tortured sight.

LXVIII
"Shadows, You Say?"

It is fitting that they roam the noon of night,
Cool darkness, or amidst stark Winter's chill,
Or ride the gust that suddenly assails
Our cheek made pallid by a sudden fright.
Their life-shells left begraved, but spirits will
Escape bone-cages—and all Reason fails
To make accounting for their stark return.
Especially in places dire, remote,
In deep woods, in old houses where foul crimes still lie.
Most deem them merely "shadows" and they yearn
To find some logic to those things we note—
Watching Things caught in the "corner of the eye."
A myriad number of the numberless dead
Hie hither after the house of flesh is shed.

Surely some are would-be avengers, cruelly slain,
Those doomed to enact their end again and again,
Residual phantoms who plague a place until
Their killers meet the Justice they deserve.
Others—so anger-laden in sinful life—
They return to us by force of evil will.
Only tormenting living souls will serve
Their purpose. And the ghostly ranks are rife
With souls of those who have not yet realized
That they are dead! Trapped, lost in that vast
Beyond, unwilling to accept the life they prized
Is gone. Some, summoned through that Gate once passed,
By thoughtless acts or Black Arts back through that Door
Are here! But what others might through that Portal pour?

Yes, They are with us here and no mere "shadows."
Those moaning winds, the "ghost lights" through the trees,
Those thoughts that something is watching, something follows,
Those semi-articulate whispers on the breeze—
They are not all illusions, tricks of nature,
Some are our oft <u>unrealized</u> Realities!
Created beings, no longer within their creature,
But free to share our world just as they please,
The legions of the lost, here left to linger,
In purposed or pained probation in our demesne,
To write upon our world with phantom finger,
To move among us—whether unseen or seen.
Among the mountainous dead there swell huge hosts
Of the disembodied "shadows" we call "ghosts."

LXIX
The Nachtkrapp
["Night Raven"]

(a Balassi Sonnet—invented form; inspired by the poetic form attributed
to Hungarian poet, Balint Balassi [1554-1594])

This horror tale is told in far-flung regions old
Of the Nachtkrapp—thing to dread!
List! Of this bugbear hear. Don't, when this fiend comes near,
Dare look at its wings or head!
One glance at absent eyes, holes in wings when it flies,
And you'll soon fall ill or dead!
After the twilight hour, it will catch and devour
Any children who are not abed,
Those who have strayed outside—those, as it may betide—
Whose path into bleak night led.

 Huge bird-thing, nature's laws defiled in beak and claws,
Rips off young limbs—then the heart
Is plucked in savage, horrid haste, and only gore
Is left in the nest. Each part
That once was human child—so late pure, meek, and mild—
GONE! This caution I impart.

LXX
The Condemned
(a Double Seguidilla Sonnet)

By stark light of fullest moon,
a figure is seen
stalking this accursed forest
to sate its grim need.
A wolf that is man
prowls each murdermoonbright night
quite bloodhungry mad.
He carries the age-old curse
of the *loup-garou.*
He yearns for sweet gibbous wane—
morrowmoon to view.
Never to be free,
yet again this night condemned
to hunt 'neath its beams.

LXXI
Crossed Planes

(a 5-5-4 Sonnet—invented type)

Most of us think "Reality" is like a shape
Of plane geometry. Of course not truly flat:
There are peaks and valleys and undulations,
But—essentially— a "surface" known. And that
Is comforting, in a way, to believe there's no escape
From the steady confluity of this form we know,
This realm we've studied from most ancient days—
Despite the sometime seeming deviations
From what we "know" is "True." Yet something says—
In the depths of our souls where odd, misgivings grow—
That perhaps (*ridiculous thought!*) there may be other planes
That sometimes intersect our "normal" world.
And some have seen these lines, all surety hurled
Out from their minds.…Then only *Horror* remains!

LXXII
They Abide!

(a Gwawdodyn [gwow-dod-in] Sonnet—invented form.
Also an Interlocking Rubaiyat Sonnet in form)

Dawn! We might forget what Night brought near.
At sunrise we may dismiss our fear.
The Light has come, and we feel safe, at "home"
In our "normal" world, back in our sphere
Of comfort. We think no specters roam
In our "now-safe" zone.…But a rhizome
Of Darkness sprouts, spreads, and tangles below—
Fed by doubts and dreads. The catacomb
Of all who lived before: They who know
All is cyclical. The day will go
As all days—down to long Night again.
Again, the Dark's somber song will grow.

The Night-Things are not gone. Yes! They remain—
Not slain—They persist as *What the Night Brings*.

PART III

THE KIMI XIBALBA

PLACE OF FEAR AND DEATH

AN EPIC VOYAGE OF HORROR
TRANSLATED FROM
THE MAYAN VERSION
OF AN OLMEC ORIGINAL

The Kimí Xibalba
("*Place of Fear and Death*")
[an Olmec voyage of Discovery and Horror]

 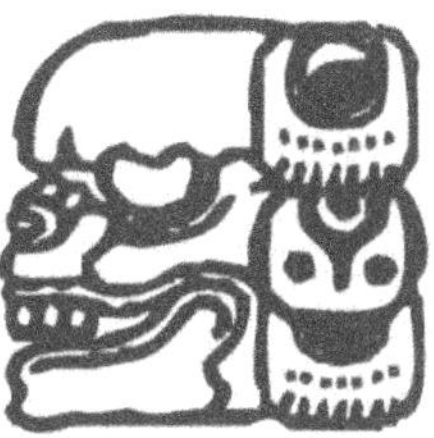

[1927 A.D. : "…a recently discovered and translated
Mayan account—derived, it contends, from a
Pre-Olmec[1] account of a terrifying voyage of discovery—circa 2000 B.C."
*Translated from the Quiché Mayan with additional following notes by
the renowned Mayanist, Dr. Sir Daniel Francis Chapman"*]

The stars were different there. The Wain[1]
Had sunk beneath the silver main.
And long we drifted at a loss,
Until we noted that a Cross[3]
Remained as constant as that Star
That served as guide in North afar.

The gods below, the gods of sky,
The gods of earth can't tell me why
I, a carver of the Heads of Stone[4],
Agreed to voyage to that zone.
Altogether, there were ten,
But ten of us—all hearty men.

We thought we had stocked food enough
Into our great, round coracle.
Too soon the Sea grew fierce and rough,
And Quixtla, our guide, our oracle,
Said we must head off to the East
And find some land—or else The Beast
Of Ocean would kill and pull us down,
Or, if we were lucky, simply drown.

We lived those many days in fear,
Striving to East with no land near.
Until, at last, we found a bay
With headlands, hills, and—far away—
A range of mountains, massive, high,
In shadowed lines against the sky.

And we found people there who said
That far to west, where dwelt The Dead—
Yea, even farther there were lands,
Small islands mid large gaps of sea
That rose up with large cliffs, black sands.
They claimed that they were sure of three.
That tale the wise Chinchorro[5] told
That—if one were strong enough and bold—
There was one island straight to West,
And if one sailed there—and was blessed
By gods and Fate—one could arrive
On that lost shore and yet survive.
But none alive had dared that chance—
To sail across that vast expanse.

"That land is where now we must go.
Departing our land, we swore we'd know
What lies Beyond the Circling Sea
And visions clear appear to me.
It is our quest, our goal to find
What lies behind that Southern Wind."
Thus, Quixtla challenged us once more.
We vowed to find that distant shore.

We rested there at least one moon,
Fed well by our friends who bid us stay.
But, stores replenished, Quixtla soon
Announced we must be on our way.

I don't think it can be expressed
In words—that voyage to the West.
How many days and nights we fought
An angry Sea! And many thought

That we were doomed. But then a calm
Set in. An East Wind seemed a balm
That soothed our minds. And clear skies blessed
The Cross that showed both South and West.
But the food ran low, ran out. And thirst
Would soon convince us we were cursed.
    Indeed, two of our number starved.
We offered their hearts to the Feathered Snake.
Thus was Kukumatza[6] served.
We left their corpses in our wake.
Our water store had just run out.
Then Xabactli gave a shout!
"Land! I see an island clear!
The next day, we were drawing near
A broad headland with towering dark
Cliffs, nearly black—a scene most stark.
But birds were wheeling overhead.
"Animals mean water," Quixtla said.
"And food. So, hasten to that shore.
    We quickly learned that, cursed once more,
The only wildlife there are rats—
Rats, moles, and birds who seemed to nest
On a smaller island just Southwest[7].
We lived on such diet a month or more,
And Quixtla made us heap up a store
Of dried and smoked rats, moles, and birds.
One day, he spoke out, "Now heed my words!
We must continue South, my men.
The stars shall tell me where and when
We reach our goal, the utmost point,
The goal we seek. I shall anoint
You and myself with waters pure
From that strange spot, that distant sea.
Then, only then—of this be sure—
We'll begin the journey home that we
Have longed for, lo! this long, long time.
We will live on in song and rhyme,
In stories that our folk will know
For thousands of moons after we go
To the Netherworld—Xibalba, far below."

The Isle of Rats and Birds

Two more of our crew had sickened and died
On that sad, small island, and we cried,
    "Quixtla, have we not gone far enough?
Through winds that whipped us, seas so rough
That we are lucky to still have breath.
Xabactli and Pongebe have both met Death.
Can six, across more unknown main,
Sail on with hope of Home again?
    "Likely as not, were already lost,
And six more lives will be the cost.
No tongues will chant our Heroes' Tale
If we all perish. We should sail
Away Northeast to home afar
And seek for that Immobile Star[6],
Letting this Cross sink far behind.
The gods be with us, we shall find
Welcome and praises from our kind."

    "Can we turn back before we reach
That point we quest for? I beseech
All of you—hold fast to your vow.
For I have a newer vision now.
I know some wondrous, eldritch wight
Lives now below that point where night
Looms over depths of deepest dark!
In dreams I hear him breathing. Hark!
And we must sail to find that place
Before we may our voyage retrace."

    With this we sighed, resigned to die,
Not knowing how or where or why.
But somewhere in that Southern Sea
I knew lay Death for them and me.
    And so, we sailed from the Isle of Birds,
Southward and westward for more than a moon.
Sick of the sea, the heat made us swoon
But Quixtla kept on, chanting unknown words.
Another man died. This time no rite.
We tossed his body over one night
When the clouds were angry and torrents fell—

And we thought his lot was less than our Hell.
One day a weird look came into the eyes
Of Quixtla, our Shaman, our Oracle wise.
"We are here!"[8] he said, with an Evil grin,
Worse than a madman's guilty of Sin.

I looked over the side to see. Then *IT* came!

"Drop buckets here! Through the Black Wave,
And over your bodies these waters lave!
Bathe in this liquid and you shall know
The Power of Him who lies below!"
     Quixtla and three others—all but me—
Bathed in the ichor of that foetid sea!
Then, staring like men who have seen great horror,
Those men were not what they'd been before!
The three knelt, bowed down, and began to groan.
Then Quixtla spoke out with words unknown.
I knew not the tongue, but shan't forget
The words he spoke. For they are set
In my mind, burned in like a brand.
Perhaps someone later will understand:
     "Ph'nglui mglw'nafh Cthulhu
R'lyeh wgah'nagl fhtagn!"[9]
     He said three times—Then he threw
Himself to the Sea. Then the others went too,
Shouting out, "He is Here. Dead, yet Dreaming!"

Then I was alone. But that Sea sounded—seeming
To boil as a kettle over high flame.
I looked over the side to see. Then *IT* came!
A huge, bulbous head with tendrils for face.
Great red eyes caught me. I cannot erase
That sight from my mind….But then all went dark!

     I know not how long I lay senseless there
In the coracle's bowels. Then thought, "Do I dare?"
But I rose up and looked out across that dread sea….
And nothing was there, but vast ocean and me.
Me, none else left in my last hope—my Ark!
I set up the sail in great haste to embark.
I thank all the gods: Earth, and Sky, and Below
That a strong South Wind began to blow.

I held a course, Northeastward and true.
Long days went passed. I began to despair
Then—much amazed!—a land that I knew.
A small island over which the birds flew.
And the Isle of Rats came into view.

I came ashore for fresh water and food—
Rats, moles, trapped birds, again my fare,

But at least I now was sure just where
I was and the way straight West, where good
Friends dwelt—The Chinchorro, our hosts
On that damned outward way, their coasts
Would be—if it were Fated—my true way
To Life, Survival—my long test past.
I sailed many days. But then—at Last!
That welcoming bay rose to my sight
On one warm, West-Wind, Full-Moon night.

They were most amazed I had returned.
And even more awed when my tale they learned.
    Their elder said, "You have sailed past Death,
Yet you return and still have breath!
None else have sailed off to that West
And returned to these shores. You must be blessed!
The gods chose you, from among all men
To see such horrors and return again."
And then he knelt down—as did they all,
And bowed his head saying, "We shall call
You 'He-Who-Has-Seen-Death-and-Returned.'"

At that, a Fire within me burned.
"I must return to the land I know
To tell my tale, let the legend grow:
There is a Dark Place, where Horror dwells
In the vast ocean, the Blackest of Hells
Lies there. And a Being most terrible sleeps,
'Neath a point in the vast sea, in Black Deeps—
A Thing most dreadful, a cosmic wight
Who wishes our bright world Endless Night!"

Those kindly people bade me stay,
But I knew I had to be on my way.
When I sailed off, they lined along
That saving shore, and they sang a song
Of blessing—a newly made one that praised
My tale of travail. And then I raised
The sail. And a wondrous following wind,
Soon left that friendly land far behind.

I sailed to the North, keeping in sight
The great mass of land that lay off to the right.
For four full moons I kept my way,
Through seas both mild and the salty spray
Whipped up by torrents and frequent gale,
But I knew that my efforts must not fail—
I must relate to my people my tale!

Then a miracle did appear,
I hove in sight of My Land!—most dear.
My people welcomed me with surprise,
They thought, as I, that living eyes
Would never again exchange a glance.
But I had returned—through Fate or Chance?

I have told my story, and I tell YOU too
That all of this tale is horribly true!
I am Ukixchan[10], and I survive!
You have heard and must keep this Truth alive.

NOTES

[1]Pre-Olmec—The Olmecs are the earliest known Mesoamerican civilization (fl. 1600 BCE-400 BCE). The Pre-Olmec culture flourished from about 2500 BCE for a millennia.

[2]The Wain—many cultures have seen the constellations of the Big Dipper and Little Dipper as the "Big Wain [or Cart]" and "Little Wain." The Dippers are important due to their stars aiding in the quick access of Polaris for navigation in the Northern Hemisphere.

[3]Clearly, a reference to the Southern Cross, the navigational constellation used in the Southern Hemisphere.

[4]Heads of Stone—Perhaps the most famous detail of Olmec culture are the enormous stone heads, quite rounded and distinctive of shape and facial features.

[5]Chinchorro—The ancient people of the Western Coastal regions of South America— (7000-1500 BCE). Almost Certainly, the tribe encountered, living in what is now Chile.

[6]Kukumatza—A variant of K'uk'ulkan, the Feathered Serpent god of the Maya.

[7]Small Island to the Southwest—the main island they must have found is now called Easter Island or Rapa Nui. The small "Island of the Birds" would be Moto Nui, a very small, spire-like island just off the coast of Rapa Nui. The Birdman Cult rituals were based on swimming to this island and safely returning with an egg from one of the nesting birds. The winner of the annual race would earn leadership for his tribe.

[8]"We are here…"—While it cannot be said for certain, given the directions and an approximation of the days spent sailing between "legs" of the voyage, the placed referenced must be very close to—if not the exact location of—Point Nemo: the oceanic Pole of Inaccessibility," or, more simply put, the point in Earth's oceans that is farthest away from any land.

[9]"Ph'nglui mglw'nafh Cthulhu R'lyeh wgah'nagl fhtagn!"—This curious, as yet untranslated, phrase has, strangely enough been attested to have also been found up into the modern era in the superstitions and rituals of various cultures.

[10] Of very few Olmec names recorded in Mayan, the king U-Kix-Chan of Palenque is one of those surviving. Likely, due to his prowess as the survivor of this voyage of discovery and horror, he became both remembered and elevated—perhaps deified.

Part III

Other Poems of the Weird, Horrific, and Supernatural

The Collection

(a Dramatic Monologue)

"You are one of the very few to see my prize
Special collection. For only a dozen eyes
Save mine have beheld this sanctum, this secret room.
So very few have been bold enough to presume
To ask of my arcane grimoire library.
     But, as Fate would have it, you are very
Welcome to enter here. The lot is small,
Containing, of course, the well-known tomes: all
Of the "standard" titles (that you must surely know),
But here, in the center of the topmost row,
Are books long-hidden, texts that are unique!
     This one, for example, set down in Ancient Greek
And Hebrew—with some hieroglyphic Egyptian—
Fits, I believe, the kind of tome your description
Suggests. It is, of all these, *that* long-lost book:
Most rare, most eldritch…most unholy! Have a look
At the binding. It is leather of the rarest skin.
And there are heinous, fell secrets held within—
Words on grim vellum writ in human blood
And illustrations that can be understood
By very few. This finely illuminated
Leaf shows an avenging Golem being created.
On this page the dead god Osiris is revived,
Brought back! Those not-to-be-uttered words survived!
This tome the ages-hid, forbidden spells imparts
To the one who is Master of the damned Demonic Arts.
     I see full well your eagerness to peruse
This and my other rarities. But you confuse
My motives—just why I brought you here.
     What? Do I detect the first faint signs of fear?
In truth, only six before you have been told
That I've found the secret of never growing old!
Unfortunately for you, the spell requires
A human sacrifice. The very fires
Of Hell are needed. And—it surely seems—much pain!
But, blessing of sorts, you'll likely go insane
Before the essence of your soul is freed
To let me live another century. My need
Keeps me from caring whether it be sin
To use you thus. Well then…let us begin."

This Side
(a Ballade Supreme, a Double Refrain)

The Unknown is dubbed the strongest form of Fear,
Attested by many souls accounted wise.
But when into the abnatural we peer,
When this world's laws are broken, we surmise
That when the thought-impossible near us nighs—
Shaking all Reason—when something "bumps" the night,
When things that can't be seen come into sight,
When all our notions of Reality fail
And something dreadful obscures Logic's light,
We're left to ponder what's Beyond the Veil.

The old tales tell that some are with us here—
Beings of legend. And our Reason vies
Against the notion such wights might be near,
Let alone extant, so our mind denies
The possibility. But our surety dies
When we encounter what just can't be Right!
And fully "Known" the reasons for our flight,
Before which things we cannot help but quail.
Those present Fears are stronger far, despite
Our need to ponder what's Beyond the Veil.

And, though most cherish Life as that most dear,
We all have wondered just what it is that lies
Beyond that Curtain that even the sagest seer
Cannot foretell—that last supreme surprise.
Though there be creeds that claim we shall arise
From this, our universal earthly plight,
We, generally, have no wish to expedite
Such transformation—head into that gale
That blows from that dim region or invite
The proof of that which lies Beyond the Veil.

Know there are things that reach Fear's greatest height!
The *Summum Terrorum* that stark horrors excite,
Things against which Reason cannot prevail,
That blight us with Evil and our days benight—
Unnatural things that lie this side The Veil!

Figures of Shadow

The "corner of the eye" will sometimes catch
A fleeting, yet moving, figure or a shape!
Often amorphous, yet sometimes we think we see
A human form. We look but cannot snatch—
In most cases—any clear view. They escape
Our searching. We ask, "How could such things be?"
Then we tell ourselves. "Merely a trick of the eyes,
An 'optical illusion,'" as it is said.
    Yet some will say they've seen these things—distinct,
Straight on. And more, much more than the surprise
Is paralyzing Fear and deepest dread.
    One theory is that these Shadow Folk are linked
As Ghosts within our realm of Life and Light,
The undeparted spirits of our dead
Moving among us, normally unseen.
    Some legends tell of a supernatural wight:
A Djinn,[1] darker than black, eyes glowing red;
"*Nalusa Chito*,"[2] as the Choctaw women keen.
    Still others say they do not come from here!
They come from *other worlds*, from *a Future Time*,[3]
Even *other Dimensions*,[4] parallel to ours!
    Most say they are aggressive, feed on our Fear.
Some tell that, incubus like, these fiends will climb
Upon a sleeping soul to steal the breath. Such powers
They have, that physical objects can be thrown
About—though they are incorporeal!
    At night they are blacker than blackest shadows,
Although they can appear by day, as is well-known.
Whether they're newly come or are primordial,
They have chosen their frightful presence to impose.
    Some say, when encountered, they seem merely curious;
Others recount aggression, actual attack
With the Shadow running at them and—*right through them!*
    Non-believers say such stories must be spurious,
Mere hallucinations, outright lies. These *Figures of Black*:
Figments of imagination to which our minds succumb.
    Yet, flickering in and out of our peripheral vision,
Those shadows at the "corner of the eye,"
Dark phantoms we've all once or often seen.
Though the thought of Shadow People meets derision,
There's evidence such doubting would belie—
In *our world, their world,* or *somewhere* in between.

Shadow Folk
(a Decima Italiana)

Darker than the darkness beneath the trees,
You may find Shadow Folk prowling the night.
At first, you'll think your eyesight can't be right,
But—when they move as men!—a fear will seize
Your very soul. You comprehend they're real!

They have been with us from the beginning.
Whence they have come or whither do they go
No one kens. And sanity's unpinning
Has been the bane of all who strive to know.
Flee! Do not seek their nature to reveal.

Beyond the Bourne
(a 5-3-4-2 Sonnet—invented form)

When one, *sans* breath, is borne beyond that bourne,
The Mystery is solved.
That one, twixt *Earthly* morn to morn,
Is not involved—
At least no more in this zone to sojourn
(So goes the common thought)
But we, the living, sometimes learn
That such is not
The case for all who go beyond *The Veil*.
Yes! Some of those souls return:
Murdered, possessed, vengeful don't fail
That *Change* to spurn.
And so full many phantom entities
Come back to plague us here—or seek their peace.

The Dreamer and the Dreaded Ones

There is a noise as of a voice
That calls beneath the sea;
And all the deep heaves, as in sleep,
With vague expectancy.
—from "The City of Darkness,"
Madison Cawein

The city not-to-be-named lies there
   Far, far beneath the waves,
Most Mankind knows not to beware,
   What it's horrid Master craves.

He dreams—though Dead! And it is said
   That from Deepest Cosmos come
Great Old Ones from that zone of dread
   Seeking Earth, again, as home.

They—and their minions—with great yearning
   Seek our world, 'though once expelled.
Oh yes! They are even now returning
   To this place where once they dwelled.

Grim Azathoth, of Chaos the King,
   The Outer Gods he rules.
Nyarlathotep, the Terrible,
   Pharoah-like who leads Earth's fools:

Benighted Legions of the Lost,
   Their senses and wits are dulled,
Not realizing the great cost,
   Into dire stupor lulled.

And Yog-Sothoth who keeps the Gate—
   Who *IS* the Gate—and knows the way
Back to our realm, where again, with hate
   Unquenched, they wend today.

Toad-like Tsathoggua, within his lair
    Awaits his prey in sloth.
No need to venture far from there
    To leave that fell cave he is loath.

Shub-Niggurath, Black Goat of the Wood,
    She with 1000 young.
All those who enter the forest should
    Fear her and her myriad sprung.

But don't forget the Dreamer deep,
    And sleeping 'neath the tides
The Pacific will not forever keep
    Dead Cthulhu—who now abides.

Strange Doo, Odd Key

Ah! They have found it!—one of many portals.
But this one gate was closed long years ago,
Hidden among the refuse that these mortals
Accumulate, store away, or idly throw
As trash—<u>or</u> simply forget amidst the attic's mess—
As this one, long since lost—now rediscovered.
They do not ken that I may gain access
Into their world, nor do they know I've hovered
Near this old passage since I last went through
Into their world. For what are fifty years to Me?
Those who now occupy the house are new.
As tenants come and go there have been three
Groups of humans living in this place,
Since those foolish warm ones opened wide the Door.
How delicious was the fear upon each face,
When they beheld me in their abject horror!

Yes! Now these new ones start to work at spells,
Asking their inane questions as they begin,
Not knowing that legions from the deepest Hells
Wait on this side each gate, yearn to go in.

In unison they ply their handiwork.
Soon they are asking what mortals should not know,
Not realizing I guide them, that I lurk
Behind the portal, that the things I show
Them are all meant to urge more queries, lure
Them to the questions that will open wide
This gateway. The words that will ensure
That I—now outside—am allowed inside
Their realm. "Is there someone here?" asks one.
I answer, "YES!" My passage coming near.
The other, "Are you human?" Answer: "NO!"
And then, "Will you give some sign or join us here?"
And with my "YES!" the threshold now is crossed,
Through plectrum's eye I glide and they are lost!
Like smoke I enter—then materialize!
Such terror! They cannot believe their eyes!
Their final cries resound in the room's gloom.
And, once again, the Ouija has led to doom.

That Time of Year
(a Burmese Ya-Du)

That time of year
That we near now
As sere leaves lie
Or cling dying
Or fly as ghosts on the wing—

Summer's last breath
O'er dry heath moans,
As Death returns.
Bale-fire burns bright.
Now yearns the Host from Beyond to cross this night.

Well we should quail
As *The Veil* tears!
Grim Tale of old
Is retold still.
Behold! Harken! Visions and voices chill!

Dark All Hallows'—
Old year's close. Fell
Shadows lengthen.
With Samhain* nigh,
We ken some will die

*NOTE: "Samhain" is pronounced in the Gaelic "saw-wen." This makes the required cross-rhyme with "ken" work in the last line.

107

Locus Horroris
(a Quatranelle*—invented form)

There is a place of Dread, of abject Horror,
Recorded only in dark, secret lore,
In grimoires unknown to most—but not to all!
If found, your soul is lost…forevermore.

Few seek it, knowing well what may befall
Their spirit if they heed stark Evil's call,
The beck of that place…as vile, grim stories tell
In grimoires unknown to most—but not to all.

Beings of Terror dire and Darkness dwell
In that forbidden zone—much worse than Hell!
Yet some have sought that place, a few have obeyed
The beck of That Land…as vile, grim stories tell.

Too late they realize they have been betrayed.
Far, far too late the horrid truths pervade
Their senses, their souls bereft of any Hope.…
Those who have sought That Land, those few who've obeyed.

The ones condemned there moan and grovel, grope
For any succor. Their world a hideous kaleidoscope.
They slump along the paths of an endless maze,
Their senses, their souls bereft of any Hope.

Though always a thick and foetid miasmic haze
Roils over that place, a bright, infernal blaze
Tended by Demons of that Nether Night
Lights the dim paths along that endless maze.

That awful place holds every abysmal wight
Ever to torment humans in their plight,
And some for whom there is no common name—
All tended by Demons of that Nether Night.

Phrike, the goddess of Fear is its beldame
Deimos, the king of Terror, Your Soul would claim.
They rule a place of Dread, of abject Horror,
A place for which there is no common name.
If found, your soul is lost…forevermore.

Slúagh na Marbh
(slu na marv)
[The Host of the Dead]
[in the Irish meter of Rannaigecht Mor]

"'Neath some Sidhe—fey, magic mounds—
Dwell the Unforgiven Dead.
Silent most nights—but fear the sounds
Should they wake!" the sage seer said.

"Beware them! Dread *Slúagh na Marbh*.
Most fell when Samhain draws nigh.
Far too near if you observe
Their curved bird-forms fearsome fly.

"Dim, grim crescents taking wing
Like a flock of grey-winged birds,
Like mere, sheer wisps wandering,
Gibbering Death's weirding words.

"None can sense them coming near—
Whether front or back or side!
Too late if one should appear
There will be no hope to hide.

"Go not near the sidhe by night.
For the fey folk dwell therein.
Seek the Good with all your might,
Avoiding the Road of Sin.

"Unforgiven, you shall meet
The horde of the *Slúagh na Marbh*
With cold welcome you they'll greet,
And in their ranks you'll serve."

Beltane

[in the Irish meter of Rannaicheacht Ghairid]
(ron-a'yach cha'r-rid)

Beltane day!
The Aos Si will hold sway.
Many great bonfires will burn.
Year turns. Summer still at bay.

Smoke, Ash, Flame—
Protect kin and kine the same.
Between twin fires and around
Mound we dance; our joy exclaim.

Just half-way
Past Ostara's blessed spring day,
Toward Litha's bright heating sun,
We run, we dance, and we pray!

Drink and food
Offered Aos Si for good.
Bright May Bush we shall betrim;
Sing hymns with magic imbued.

Summer's Dawn!
The chill nights of Spring are gone
Drive the cattle out to graze.
Now the days for foal and fawn.

La Bête du Gévaudan
(a Dizain)

A foul beast, a most ferocious terror,
Stalked the verdant region of Gévaudan,
Killed and devoured many a wayfarer.
A young shepardess' death—how it began.
Nearly 500 slain ! This scourge of man,
Woman, and child—heinous, wolf-like and wild—
Left bodies with torn throats, corpses defiled!
For more than three years was its horrid reign—
This dire wolf, werewolf, or man of the wild.
Until by silver bullet it was slain.

The Kannibaali:
A Finnish Horror Tale

"Brother join me in the rune song;
Sister, clasp my hands in chanting;
In our rocking back and forward,
Paraphrase the truth I'm telling.*
You will feel it through your fingers.
It is not some idle prattling.
Listen to my tale of horror;
Give an ear to what I utter.
Brothers, sisters please believe me;
It is not a myth I'll tell thee.
In this cold and cruel country;
On the poor soil of our Northland,
There are beings dire and dreadful,
Wights who roam who are All Evil.
Such are cruel, undead vampyrri
And the werewolf, ihmissusi;
Of course the ghosts, the fantomeja;
Many monsters, hirviöitä.
But the tale I now will chant out,
Singing song of sorrows countless—
This my long-dead father sang me,
Clasping both my hands in his hands.*
Rocked we back and forth together
As this grim tale he related;
And the truth flowed through his fingers,
I could feel the Fear remembered,
As we moved like waves of ocean,
Lapping on the Shore of Sorrow,
Crashing on the sharp-rock shingle."

'List, my son, unto my story,
Hear, my boy, my tale of terror.
I was only thirteen winters,
Just your age when this horror happened!
I had gone out from the village,
Left the safety of our homestead,
I was out to prove my manhood,
Bring back game to quell our hunger.
But I strayed too far in hunting,
And I found myself benighted.
But I soon learned that the darkness,
Night itself was not the horror.
In the woodland deep I saw it!
Glow of greenish light approaching.
Hid I then among the bushes,
When a noise of footfalls coming
And a growling sound foreboding,
Uttered by whate'er approached me,
Filled me with a sudden terror,
And I tried to stop my breathing
Seeking then to be most silent
As the Thing stopped close beside me.
I dared not look, at first, upon it;
Dared not lift my face to see it.
For it paused and grunted deeply,
And it sniffed the breeze about it!
Thank the gods, it kept on walking;
But I sensed it dragging something!
To my horror, when I dared look up,
I saw that it dragged a dead man!
That green glow was all about it,
Seemed to come from deep within it.
Why I did not run I know not;
Something in my soul compelled me.
And I followed that foul being;
At first, I could not see its features,
As it walked the path before me,

But I saw its giant stature,
Taller than a man by half!
Soon it came into a clearing,
Dragging the poor corpse behind it.
Then it dropped its dreadful burden.
And I had to stop from screaming

When I first beheld its features!
When I saw the fiery eyeballs
And beheld the fangs and fingers
Tipped with claws like curving knifeblades!
Then it started in to eating
That poor man. A Kannibaali!
A Corpse-Eater—ruumissyöjä!
Was this Thing I had encountered!
With knife talons tore the torso,
Lifted out the gory entrails,
Gorged upon the poor man's organs,
Ripped the limbs from off the body,
Cracking bones made awful noises!
At that I sprang from where I'd hidden
Heard I the Thing arise and follow;
 Necrovore was coming for me!
Never ran one any faster;
How I lived I cannot answer.
Winding through those forest pathways,
Growling on the wind diminished,
Then I came into my village.
Only one, an Elder, heard me,
Nodding 'Yes' at my grim story.
All the rest thought I was crazy.
But I swear my tale's a true one;
You, my son, you must believe me.
When you hunt the deepest forest,
Be wary of the weird around you.
Stray not, stay not past the nightfall!
Beings nowhere close to human
Share our world! You must beware!'

"This the tale my father told me;
This the chant that chills my blood.
Brothers, Sisters, please believe me.
There are Evils far more fearsome:
Things worse than your darkest nightmares;
Things beyond our comprehension.
They are not mere stuff of legend;
They are real—and mean our Ending!"

When the Suns Set Over Carcosa
(a terzanelle)

In Lost Carcosa somber shadows spread.
The cloud banks break against the shore.
The King in Yellow rules o'er the massed undead.

The story's more than frightful, ancient lore.
When twin suns set behind the loathsome lake
And the cold clouds roil and swirl upon the shore—

Then Evil Wights, Night's Children will awake!
Strange moons, black stars rise darker than the sky
When twin suns sink behind that loathsome lake,

Abandon Hope—for it is time to die.
If not already dead and in the thrall
(As strange moons, black stars bedeck the sky)

Of that King in Yellow rags who rules them all.
The songs of the Hyades cannot be heard
By those already doomed and in His thrall.

A horrid Fate upon all is conferred,
When in Lost Carcosa somber shadows spread.
The songs of the Hyades cannot be heard,
The Yellow King awakes! All Hope is fled.

A Forest Encounter

At the far southern tip of Illinois
The Shawnee Forest spreads across the land,
From the Ohio to the Mississippi.
Sprawling, thick woods and many a tributary
Creek or river, and rolling hills have spanned
That country centuries before, when, as a boy,
 I roamed that region, careless in my youth,
Ranging near Ripple Hollow, east of McClure.
   I loved those hills, those broad creeks, and those trees.
But one day, straying late, I learned the truth!
Call me crazy if you want to, but I'm sure
I saw the Thing. First a stench upon the breeze,
And then…a panther, blacker than any night—
But fully ten feet long! That Thing ain't right!

Of course, I ran—but not at first. I froze
When I looked into those red and glowing eyes.
The Thing had killed a white-tail and it fed
Upon the gory carcass of the deer.
I can't describe the sight, the utter fear
That overcame me or the horror of those
Huge, long fangs that ripped. "I'm dead,"
I thought.
                It's only a thing that flies
Could flee from that glance my way that meant,
"You're next," faster than I through that wild wood.
I ran and stumbled through thickets 'till I was spent.
But something kept me moving. Then I stood
In a clearing, but could still hear distant growls.
I tell you the Black Cat's there—and it still prowls!

The Seeker's Lament

(a villanelle)

I yearn to dream a place where all is bright,
The darkness shattered by a strong dawn sun,
But nightmares show a place of Endless Night.

I long to glimpse these glowering stars take flight,
Fleeing—before the great Day-Star to run.
I seek—in dreams—a place where all is bright.

Sleeping, I delve the depths, the Sky's great height,
Looking for gleaming Hope—but I find none.
My night terrors travel to Eternal Night.

I know now that deliverance' chance is sleight—
Knew it as soon as these visions had begun!—
My wakings too find no place were all is bright.

Must I resolve myself to this sad plight?
Can this wretched Darkness never be undone?
Can I escape this land of Endless Night?

Nay! Since I spoke those words—a Forbidden Rite!
The Gate is open! Demon wights have come—and won!
Though I might seek a place where all is bright,
Night Wraiths are Real! I'm doomed to Endless Night!

Ghostly Glossary
(A Terzanelle le Grande, invented form—
A "triplication" of the standard Terzanelle)

Phantoms, spectres, ghosts of many kinds
Are with us here in this our "normal" realm.
No mere imagined figments of our minds.

They have the power to touch us, overwhelm!
We mortals left behind have cause for dread.
They join us from their paranormal realm.

Most are the disembodied spirits of the dead.
They still have power, although they've ceased to live!
We mortals left behind have cause for dread.

Some come, Residual Phantoms, to relive
Tragic truths, attached to a haunted spot.
They still have powers, although they've ceased to live.

A hopeless suicide, foul murder forgot,
Most heinous crimes have forced them to remain,
'Till tragic truths are revealed at the spot.

They seek revenge, or to remove some stain—
No doubting they wish us to know they're there.
Most heinous crimes have forced them to remain.

Another kind are the Poltergeists. Beware!
They plague the humans who would dare to stay.
(No doubting *They* wish us to know they're there).

Noisy, restless, mischievous these spirits fey
Arouse great fear in places they deem "home."
They plague the people who would dare to stay.

Not all appear in human form. For some—
The Shadow Shapes or Orbs and eerie lights
Arouse stark terror in places where they roam.

Will-o-the-Wisps; "Ghost Gleams"; dim, formless frights
Are yet another group of spectres grim—
These Shadow Shapes and Orbs and eerie lights.

And one may meet—by day or when all is dim—
Objects or Places with spirits of their own!
These are but two more groups of phantoms grim.

A box! a doll! a house! a hotel! It's known
That Evil Essences can infest such Things!
These objects or places have spirits of their own.

A weirding horror the Doppelgänger brings.
Their human counterpart will quake in fear!
The essence of Evil dwells within such things.

The human twin is blamed, though nowhere near
The heinous actions done by bloody ghost.
The living counterpart will quake in fear.

And numbered in this Legion of the Lost:
All the grim Evils and fell Wights of Fright
Are in the van of all that ghastly host.

Yea! All the myriad "Things that Bump the Night"—
Phantoms, Spectres, Ghosts of many kinds.
These *Things of Dread* give ample cause for fright.
No mere imagined figments of our minds.

Shiryo
(a haibun)

my lover's *shiryo*
has visited me each night
since the "accident"

He wishes me to join him in that Other World, that place no
living soul is permitted to see. He beckons, a faint spirit, a *yurei*.
So far, I have resisted, and I am saddened that I now fear him
who I had loved so long…

The Lurker of Göbekli Tepe

For thirteen thousand years I've lain in wait,
Marked in their icons by an **H**, "*The Gate*"
I am—but also *IT* who has passed through
That portal from the distant stars to instigate
Dichotomies of Doom. These ancients knew
To link the aspects of my power. They'd hew
These odd, imperfect H-shapes into stone.
Ages later, world-wide, more civilized people drew
More accurate images of Me as *The One*,
Staff in each hand. I'm variously shown
As Egypt's dual-sceptered king; as "*Bab-ilu*,"
"God Gate," to the Akkadians; and none
Other than *Viracocha* whom the Incas drew
Or etched into the rock.... *The One* who knew—
As he who was the "Master of Time and Space"—
The ages that this small world would go through,
The fates I planned for this poor human race!

Those ancient people buried deep this place,
But now these mortals excavate again.
And, though they dig at such a slothful pace,
Though buried deep for long, do I remain
Master of their Chaos, Insanity, and Pain.
And, even dulled, my powers have been their bane.

They dig! My many-circled sigil will be revealed
They thought I'd die when my temples were concealed.
I wait, full ready to resume my reign.
What horrors I shall work—when I am free again!

After the Gloaming

(a Catena Rondo—
form invented by Robin Skelton)

Grey gloaming glooms and nightfall fleetly nears.
As umbras spread, old legends we should heed
Of storied wights that roam and slay and feed.
Grey gloaming glooms and nightfall fleetly nears.

As unbras spread, old legends we should heed
Of ghosts and vampires, werewolves, ghouls and more
That use the night—foul beings to abhor.
As umbras spread, old legends we should heed.

Of ghosts and vampires, werewolves, ghouls and more,
Most think of them as fiction to affright,
Mere stuff of legend, born in the mind's dark night—
Where dwell ghosts, vampires, werewolves, ghouls and more.

Most think of them as fiction to affright.
But they are with us! Here in our demesne
They move quite freely—Thank God they're seldom seen!
Still, most think them a fiction to affright.

Yes, they are with us here in our demesne.
Ghosts of each ilk will make their presence known,
Phantoms no longer bound to flesh and bone.
These spirits are with us here in our demesne.

Ghosts of each ilk will make their presence known:
Condemned by Evil, Earth-bound is their lot,
Beguiling specters, those who haunt a spot.
Ghosts of each ilk will make their presence known.

Condemned by Evil, Earth-bound is their lot.
Such are the vampire brood, the cursed Undead,
nosferatu, foul *strigoi*—by Man's blood fed.
Condemned by Evil, Earth-bound is their lot.

Such are the vampire brood, the cursed Undead,
Monsters of Darkness, fell foes of humankind,
Spawn of dread Dracul his breed to Hell assigned.
Such are the vampire brood, the cursed Undead.

Monsters of Darkness, fell foes of humankind,
So too those doomed to change with each full moon,
The wretched werewolves for whom death's a boon—
Monsters of Darkness, fell foes of humankind.

The lycanthropes transform with each full moon.
They prowl the night and, ravenous, they feed
On those unwary. Beware them! Heed my rede.
These humans *reshape* as wolves with each full moon.

They prowl the night and, ravenous, they feed—
Defying all of this world's Natural rules—
The ghastly, grim, and gory gluttonous ghouls!
They prowl the night and on cadavers feed.

Defying all of this world's Natural rules
Are demons, bogies, all Creatures of the Night.
If met, your fate may be far worse than Fright.
Such things defy all this world's Natural rules.

* * *

Grey gloaming glooms and nightfall fleetly nears.
As umbras spread, old legends we should heed
Of storied wights that roam and slay and feed.
Grey gloaming glooms and nightfall fleetly nears.

Lob

Soon after he bought the Carolina manse—
Not only in the cellar (to be expected),
But throughout, in upstairs rooms, in attic loft,
Were a thousand bugs. Large Wolf Spiders would dance,
Skittering across the floors. The place infected,
Especially those eight-eyed things with their soft,
Round, furry bodies and their hideous form
Repulsed him. They had claw-tipped legs to clutch,
And quick—too quick!—and seeming keen of sight!

To free the ancient dwelling of the swarm—
Such infestation would not do, and such
Was his abhorrence of these freaks of fright—
He called exterminators in to end the plague.
That seemed, at first, to solve the critter curse.
But—within two weeks—one night, while reading late
In the large study, there was a noise! Quite vague
At first, but soon a scraping sound. Then worse!
A loud CRASH! He had to investigate.

Descending the cellar stairs, lantern in hand,
A heavy brass fireplace poker in the other,
He noted the noise had ceased. This only stoked his dread.

Revealed in one corner—no way to comprehend
The size of what must have been the Spider Mother!
Eight huge eyes glinted, bulging from its head.

The shrieking in his mind drowned out his scream
That echoed through the mansion. For his ears
Caught only the scraping of the monster's race
From the old coal cellar door, black eyes agleam,
A thing of perfect horror far past all fears!
Impossibly fast across that dungeon's space!

The foremost legs, tipped with great grasping hooks,
Had caught him firmly! Oh! So very quickly!
No "fur" but coarse wires grew from that huge glob.
   Somehow, his mind went back to the glanced-at books
On the species, as its maw spewed ichor thickly
Over his numbing body. The heinous lob
Would liquify his form—then drink him in!
Suck up his essence in a few days' time!
"Exterminate!"…his thought…then all thoughts did stop.

   Only a pool of goo where the man had been,
Along with rather curious, putrid slime,
Remained as hint of the giant attercoppe.
None who investigated could ever explain
The large hole in the cellar's farthest wall.
All wondered why any tenant would remain
In such a house where so many creatures crawl!
For they were thick—foul pests of every sort!—
Most awful the myriad spiders…by report.

The Nuckelavee:
Monstrous Wight of the Orkneys
[in an approximation of some of the meters of *The Gododdin*]

The Orkney Isles folk tell of a Terror
That all should beware who venture there.
Some summer safety when rules the Sea's Mother*,
Or if rain is falling—that is another
Thing that wards off the Nuckelavee,
Since it dwells beneath the briny sea.
Nor can it cross any freshwater way.
Finding a stream may save you one day.
One more thing: by stench of burning seaweed,
As done to make kelp, one might also be freed.
For it hates that foul smell and will not come near.
In this way too you may stave off stark Fear.

But if on the land you encounter this beast,
Know that it plans on your corpse to feast.
If its long arms can grab you, it will pull you down
To its den in the sea, and surely you'll drown.
Simply the sight of it can bring your death
Through absolute horror. Its poisonous breath
Kills kine and blights crops as it roams far and wide,
A scourge to all life o'er the broad countryside.

Few live to describe its hideous shape.
Some have been found…final-scream mouth agape.
For its form is most hideous. **The Nuckelavee**
Is the worst of the horrors that come from the sea:
A skinless man's torso attached to the back
Of a monstrous red horse that also does lack
Any flesh! And this monster, Red Evil aglow,
Through raw muscles and veins a black blood does flow!
The head of the horse-part has only one eye,
Cyclopean horror that on fin-feet can fly
Through the waves, but has hooves on the land —
A mutation of form we do not understand.
On a neck that seems broken bobs 'round huge man-head,
Ten times normal size, giant skull of one dead.

And a black awful ichor and pestilent breath
Comes forth from that mouth—a true Maw of Death.
And the arms of the "rider" hang down near the ground
To snatch up its victim if a human be found.
With huge hands, long fingers and dagger-like claws,
The Nuckelavee defies all Nature's Laws.

So, if you'd go walking the shore of the seas
That rise with huge whitecaps around the Orkneys
Be wary and watch that you don't chance to see
This Horror from Hell—The Nuckelavee,
For seeing this man-horse with red glowing eye,
Huge man-mouth agape—you most surely will die.
Your only hope: quickly find a fresh stream
Your life in its waters you just might redeem.
Far better to shun, when fierce Teran** holds sway
And the Mither of the Seas* has gone on her way,
Until the summer brings safety back 'round,
Scant help from the Nuckelavee might be found.

Few live to describe its hideous shape…

Notes on "The Nuckalavee"

*The Sea Mother or "Mither o' the Sea" was the spirit of summer and the warmer half of the year. During the time she held sway, the Nuckelavee has held in check beneath the waves.

**Teran was the antithesis of the Mither o' the Sea, the spirit of winter and the colder half of the year. During his time, the Nuckelavee was free to roam on the earth.

And so, there was a constant battling between these two forces, dividing the year into the relatively safe warmer half and the far more dangerous colder half.

The Nuckelavee...
Is the worst of the horrors that come from the sea:
A skinless man's torso attached to the back
Of a monstrous red horse that also does lack
Any flesh!

Mgae Aswang
Aswangs: Malevolent Ghosts of the Philippines
(in Tanaga Meter)

Aswangs! There are five dread kinds.
All are ghosts. Pure Evil finds
You if one you chance to meet,
Death's a thing you will not cheat.
***
As Vampire, it seems to be
A woman of great beauty.
Not through teeth it takes your blood,
But through pointed tongue its food.

It lives among human kind—
Often does a husband find,
Slowly drain away his life,
As a horrid, monstrous wife.

Or else it uses the home
As mere hideout, far to roam,
Seek blood from those far away,
To return by break of day.
***
On your viscera will suck
They who dwell in forest deep
Through its tube tongue it will pluck
Out your guts while you're asleep.

Seemingly a woman fair,
Long-haired, and lovely by day,
By night grows wings, takes to air,
Leaving its lower body where

None will find it, safely hid,
The upper torso flies far,
Seeking prey, and God forbid!
Finds where pregnant women are.

Its ghastly food—the child within!—
The Gut Sucker's greatest sin.
Beware! Beware! This foul wight.
They who fly and feast by night.
***

The Weredog is one to fear.
Not living with humankind,
But can as nomad draw near
In human guise—prey to find.

At midnight it shifts its shape
From man to dog. No escape
If you see this fiend most strange—
Meet it after ghostly change.

If met past the midnight hour
It will kill and quick devour.
You will know your time has come,
Nevermore to see your home.
***

Aswang Witch will foully curse
Those who anger her. Much worse
Than Death might well be your plight
If you cross this wizened wight.

Out from every orifice
Will ooze insects, bones, or rice!
Outside the village they dwell,
Fear the outskirts! Gates of Hell!

Aswang Witches power is more
Than other witches. Abhor
Both kinds but the former kill.
Shun the plain witch with a will.

131

Witch Aswangs have eyes like cat,
Weird pupils—each like a slat.
This is how to know this ghost.
Earn her wrath—then you are lost!
***

Aswang Ghouls! Perhaps the worst
Horrid is this breed accurst!
On our corpses does it feast!
Such the food of this foul beast.

Hid near graveyards, they will prey
On the dead. After the day
Falls and the black night comes on
Ghastly feeding before dawn.

Foul of smell, face of horror,
Heinous fiends that feast on gore!
Sharp of fang with fearsome claws,
Breaking all of Nature's Laws.

Hid when burials are fresh,
Waiting to devour dead flesh!
Most abhorrent this ghoul ghost,
Preying on the dead and lost.
***

These then are the five aswang
Known from folk tales and grim song.
Awful ghosts that plague us here.
Giving us great cause for Fear.

Väinämöinen

(in an approximation of *Kalevala* meter)

I will sing of Väinämöinen,
Chant the lore of that great hero,
How he was Ilmatar's offspring,
Son of the great primal goddess.
Thirty years and seven hundred,
As she floated in the great sea,
Ere the Earth was fully shapen,
Did she hold him in her belly.
All the wisdom of the Ages,
Väinämöinen had within him.
Then, at last, after long praying
To the sun, the moon, the Great Bear,
Was he born and swam off landward.

But the land was dry and barren,
So—with pieces of the Sampo—
Aided well by Pellervoinen,
Did the Earth spring forth with bounty,
Did Life spread wide o'er the country.

Then did he begin his singing,
Bard of Order over Chaos,
With his beauteous voice he chanted,
So creating Kalevala
And the lineage of that great king,
Leaders in the Land of Heroes.

Väinämöinen's voice so mighty,
Magical was hero's chanting.
Thus, the villain Joukahainen,
Rival of great Väinämöinen,
Was by power of song bemired,
Swallowed in the boggy depths.
And the Great Pike did he vanquish,
Made a harp out of its jawbones.

Finally, he left this mid-world,
On the shore of the vast Ocean,
Sang himself a boat of copper,
Sailed away from mortal lands.
But he promised a returning
Prophesied that he'd be needed,
His great powers once more called for.

Katabasis
(a Rhymed *Sestinelle* with Full Refrains—invented form)

There are dread places few would dare to go:
Regions that *Reason* rend, loci that strain
Belief, that one's sense of *The Real* wholly defy.
Yet—far more horrible!—*some* lie nearby,
Places of Terror, far, far from the mundane.
Most dreaded is that Realm that lies below.

Most dreaded is that Realm that lies below.
If—of that nether journey—you would know,
Know that it is a strange and tangled skein
Of mysteries both awful and arcane,
Of revelations that will damage and defy
All current beliefs upon which you rely.

All current beliefs upon which you rely
Will be obscured by an umbrageous shadow,
Will fall 'neath *Eldritch Visions* you shall descry.
Lore of that zone began so long ago
That none can say the age of that refrain—
The tales most terrible of that domain.

In tales most terrible of that domain
Might be some inklings that demystify—
Some of that knowledge…if you still are fain?
Such stories, full of wisdom, full of woe,
Legends that will vistas bleak bestow,
If still into such knowledge you would pry.

If still into such knowledge you would pry,
Inanna/Ishtar took that path of pain
Through Seven Gates, then sentenced by sister-foe,
Ereshkigal, the Queen of all who die,
To stay forever there, e'en Death did she know,
Before allowed to reach Life's Realm again.

Before allowed to reach Life's Realm again,
Orpheus, whose lyre could mystify,
Beguile all animals, e'en Hades overthrow,
Sought to retrieve his wife—but all in vain.
Odysseus called with blood the shades to draw nigh,
To tell the woes endured in that Land of Shadow.

To find the woes endured in that Land of Shadow,
Aeneas too sought out that dismal plane,
Once more to meet his father. And thereby
He learned of that Place of Death—although
No joy it brought. Many would know *Tomorrow*,
The End of that Last Caravanserai.

As has been known for aye—all, *All* will die.
All lives shall wane, none may shun this bane.
Yet few care to go to that dread Realm below.

Cursed Mansion

(an Unrhymed, *Extended* Sestinelle with Incremental Refrains
—an invented form)

The legend had it that the place was cursed,
That hilltop manse above the river town—
A hulking giant looming over all
That shadowed valley and the shaded stream
That rent the hills asunder and the gloom
That settled even days that should be bright.

Yea, even on the days that should be bright,
The town was dismal, dim. Sunlight dispersed
Through mists that made folk *say "An awful doom
Awaits us. And that mansion looking down
Upon us is the source! For we all deem
It must be haunted!"* The place had them in thrall.

Certain it was it had power to enthrall.
From out a central hall to left and right
Stretched out long monstrous wings that made it seem
Like arms that would grab and crush them, but the worst
Thing about that horrid place was the startling frown
The huge doors' "maw," twin window "eyes" that loom.

For two arched windows, large, weird-lit, did loom
Above the town. And their light did appall
The townsfolk. For the owners were all gone!
All dead a century before! So a great fright
Befell the valley people. But none had durst
Go up the hill to see what made that gleam!

"I'll find the reason for that eerie gleam,"
Young Thomas said. *"That house is but a tomb,
The evil dwellers dead. No matter how accursed
The place may seem, a seeming horror is all
There be. Which I shall prove this very night!"*
Then he set off—beneath a blood-red moon.

The ancient path beneath that bloody moon,
Forsaken long and brambled o'er did seem
The very Road to Hell. And he, in spite
Of his brave boast, to see the weird manse loom
Before him—dim-lit window "eyes," fear did befall
His spirit. As if in Evil he'd been immersed!

In *Evil* both Pure and Dark was he immersed.
And suddenly, beneath that ruddy moon,
The huge "maw" doors swung open and withal
There came strange shapes—as in a Nightmare Dream—
The kind in which monstrous, horrific things subsume
All sense of what is "Real." *"This can't be right!"*

Young Thomas' soul screamed out—*"This can't be right!"*
Of the Things spewing from that "mouth," the worst—
With rows of eyes the red moon did illume,
With dripping fangs and claws of onyx hewn—
Was on him in a trice. His dying scream
Was cut short. Such was Thomas' horrid fall.

The valley folk were sure of Thomas' fall
For they had heard his cry cut through the night.
All knew, in that dim town by darkling stream,
The lad had been the last—*e'en tho' the first*—
To dare to test that place that loomed aboon
Their village. All knew he'd met his doom.

They live in gloom. Their end comes soon. That place *is* cursed.
That shaded stream nor heeds their plight—nor mournful call.

The Firefox

(a legend of Finland in *Kalevala* meter)

I will chant a Finnish legend.
Listen as my word-store opens,
and I choose the proper measures,
set before you an amazing
tale the people tell by hearthside.
    I will tell you of the Firefox,
the strange beast called tulikettu,
roaming in our northern forests.
Very few are blessed to see it.
Black, it hides well in the shadows
during day—but in the nighttime
its fur sparks and twinkles brightly,
so you'd think its coat was burning.
Hunters rare who have its leather;
    Scarce the ones who've trapped the Firefox.
They are granted lifetime riches.
When they brush the pelt of wonder,
weird light glimmers from that fox-skin.
When the Firefox runs through woodlands;
when it brushes bushes, branches;
then it makes the revontulet,
Northern Lights, the magic Fox Fires!
    Now you know about this marvel,
wonder of our wild North Woodlands.

The Minstrel
(a ballad)

Through the rugged Scottish Highlands,
  Amid heathered hill and glade,
I roam the rugged backroads
  'Tis there I ply my trade.

I'm a magic master minstrel.
  It should come as no surprise
That my mystic songs and singing
  Have great power to mesmerize.

When I play upon my black-stained lute,
  Sounding chords mysterious, deep,
Though the folk be awed and wakeful,
  I can lull them all to sleep.

As I chant forth special verses,
  None suspect my human guise
Or remember the trance infernal
  Upon waking. Nor do they surmise

That, when one of their pitiful number
  Within the week lies dead,
Young and healthy—too soon to slumber—
  That I was the Thing of Dread.

For I favor the blood of young ones
  To fulfill my evil need.
I savor the flavor of hearty blood
  When I have the urge to feed.

Yes, more than a singer of tales am I,
  An Evil Wraith most dire.
I roam these Highlands and ply my trade—
  Monstrous minstrel…a grim vampire.

The Dulachan:
The Headless Horseman of Ireland
(an adaptation of the Irish form of the Seadna)

Dulachan, demon most fearsome!
Seeing it fills folk with dread.
Riding a black steed, this horror–
Holds a bleeding, gory head!

Held high in its hand–this demon,
Dire rider, gruesome wight of fright–
Is its own head! Eyes always seeking
Its prey through the darkest night.

Foul flesh of that face is rotting.
It roams on its nightly trip;
Gan Ceann ("Without a Head") horseman.
A human spine is its whip!

But sometimes it drives Death's Wagon
Decked out in funeral trim:
The lamps are skulls lit by candles,
The wheel's spokes are thighbones grim.

The Wagon is covered over
In worm-eaten human skin.
It drives with its head tucked under
It's arm—with ear-to-ear grin.

Where're *Dulachan* stops riding,
Somebody is doomed to die.
And if it's your name that's mentioned,
Your soul is quite soon to fly.

Some say that a golden object
Can force this horror to go.
Put no trust in this old saying.
Whether true? Don't seek to know.

NOTE:

The Fox River is a 202-mile-long tributary of the Illinois River, flowing from southeastern Wisconsin to Ottawa, Illinois and its confluence with the larger water. The Fox runs along to the west of both Milwaukee and Chicago, through rural areas and suburbs. It flows through Elgin, Illinois, current home of the present poet.

Many sites along the length of the Fox are famous for hauntings. Towns on either side of the river valley have legends of ghosts and inexplicable occurrences. The following poems chronicle only a few of these legends.

The Horror of Devil's Cave
(vicinity of what is now Aurora, Illinois)

Waubonsee, Chief of the Potawatomie
Whose name translates "He Causes Pallor,"
After an act of gruesome, bloody valor—
The Osage were the enemy, and he
Snuck into their camp one moonless night to claim
Several lives and scalps, escaping at "Break of Day"
(Another meaning of his name, some say).
In either case, this legend brought him fame.

Against America in Tecumseh's feud,
A leader against Harrison at Tippecanoe,
He later changed his mind, and so he threw
His tribe against Blackhawk when wars renewed.
Indeed, he banned his warriors from shedding blood
Of settlers in the lands now Illinois.
He thought that path the best for his tribe's good.
But one brave did that hope for peace destroy.
Muktemnedo, the "Black Spirit," massacred
A family of white settlers—despite the ban.
And so, he became outcast, an exiled man
As soon as Waubonsee the story heard.

All thought the banished one was gone for good,
Up with the Ojibway beyond the Greatest Lake—
Beyond wide Kitcheegumee to the Northern Wood.
But that would prove to be a great mistake.

It was late autumn when *the Evil* came
And members of the tribe were cruelly killed.
The dead were many—scalped and mutilated—
But, just as horrible, the tale that some related
Of seeing a Glimmering Ghost where blood was spilled,
A frightful sight!—this demon the one to blame.
A glowing shape would suddenly appear,
Manlike, eerie, then…just as suddenly
Be gone! And now they saw nobody near!
The spectre kept on murdering in a spree.

A group of stalwart braves Waubonsee led,
Hunting to find and end his tribe's new plight.
They hid in the brush. And then they saw the light.
The Gleaming One, the phantom fiend most dread.
But Waubonsee saw it was all a trick
When the thing emerged from out the forest thick.
Foxfire had been used to cast the weirding glow,
To make a mere man monster. He would throw
A blanket 'round himself to disappear.
All this Waubonsee saw. The man drew near.
Behold! It was Muktemnedo, the banished man.
With war whoops the men rose up; the villain ran.
He fled into a cave in a ravine,
Hoping that he was safe, had not been seen.
But that cave had become his prison—*no way out.*
The band had followed. Then Waubonsee did shout:
"You are traitor to your tribe, and your return
To murder your own kin means you will burn!"

They piled up branches at the cave's dark door
Set them alight, and the deadly flames did soar.
The villain could not withstand the heat and smoke,
And from that cave's black maw he screamed and broke!
But could not get past the blaze. He tripped and fell
Into that inferno—*no less hot than Hell.*
His shrieks of agony echoed through the dark.
But the legend says his soul did not embark!
His black spirit haunts Devil's Cave unto this day.

Especially in late autumn, so they say,
Far louder than the Fall Wind's howling breath—
Come dreadful wails of excruciating Death!

Munger Road

There are still those who dare it…The Tale of Munger Road.
Local high-schoolers mostly, or young folks on a lark.
The story of the tragedy and its ghosts!…that is the goad.
And so, they drive out to the tracks and park—long after dark.

. . .

The day is stormy, snowy; the bus stalls on the rails,
Filled with forty children, the eldest get out to push,
The driver sees the train, the starter fails and fails,
And then the Beast is on them, howling in a rush!
And all are dead, including the valiant few whose shove
Was just not quite good enough. Their young souls are above.

. . .

So, some drive out and park there, astride that fated rail.
And put the car in neutral, but they don't forget to spread
Talcum or baby powder—on this point they must not fail.
The challenge is to wait there—for a train *and for the dead!*

And soon they see the coming light, coming near and nearer—
A hooting, howling cyclops in unstoppable career
And most start up their car again and drive away in fear.
But some, the rare few bold enough to stay and stare and wait,
Have lived! And they attest the tale is true—how they dodged fate:
As trains approach a crossing, the engineers all know
Long…long…short…long the train whistle to blow.
But those that dared the challenge of haunted Munger Road
All tell a tale of marvel, a saving grace bestowed:

Before that coming train can claim its gruesome toll
The car will start to move and—amazingly—will roll
Clear of the tracks. Yes, still the eerie legend stands:
On the car's rear, powdered bumper are seen…
prints of many tiny hands.

Elvira: Ghost of The Woodstock Opera House

Though a small town, the village of Woodstock
Boasts an Opera House of widespread fame.
But some say they have suffered quite a shock,
For both audience members and some actors claim
That there are "performances" not on the stage.
Actors who have gone on to become great names:
Paul Newman, Orson Welles, and Geraldine Page;
Tom Bosley, Betsy Palmer—some attest that games
Are being played by one particular ghost.
The lobby doors mysteriously close and open;
Stage props are moved. But of weird things the most:
Seat DD113, spring-loaded, lies flat—but then
Pops up as if a patron, leaves…unhappy with the play,
"Elvira" she's called. Mere legend? Who can say?

A Matter of Degrees:
Ghosts of the Stickney Mansion

Not far outside Bull Valley, a tiny town
In Northeast Illinois, west of the Fox,
A mansion was built, a place of great renown
Due to the tales of supernatural shocks
That have attached to that oddly structured house.
    For the Stickneys, George and Sylvia, you see—
Devout spiritualists—a theory did espouse
That spirits both good and evil could be caught
In corners of ninety degrees and could not free
Themselves from such. Thus, any spirits brought
Across through the many séances they planned
Must have clear pathways back across The Veil.
    And so, they commissioned a builder with the demand
That every internal corner—without fail!—
Be laid out nowhere close to being square.
    This he complied with almost perfectly,
Except in one inside corner near the stair
Its angle off 90 by only one degree.
    Their house completed, the séances began,
And it is claimed many spirits entered there.
Although, today, most think the tale less than
Credible—it's true there might be reason to beware.
    For one day, in that corner—too close to right—
George Stickney's heart stopped beating and he fell
Down dead. Since then, other reasons to affright
Might well be due to some demon trapped from Hell,
Unable to escape that corner of dread.
    You see, the widow Sylvia kept on holding
Her séances summoning spirits of the dead.
Her fame grew, Medium Sylvia's trances unfolding
Messages from various loved ones now passed on.
The upstairs ballroom was the séance room.
    Eventually, Sylvia too was dead and gone.

Since then, both Stickney's in the tomb
Strange things have been reported of that place:
Sounds of movement upstairs, and whisperings,
Steps on the stairways, the sight of a hideous face,
Doors opening and closing, strange odors, and things
Moved about from place to place, a bodyless shout!
    The Stickney's had ten children. Three only
Lived to adulthood. And when their line ran out,
The house was put up for sale, still in a lonely
Spot, not so far now from the little village.
    The fellow who took the real estate photo
Swears that the house was empty, but a visage
Is seen, a woman in white, at the window
Upstairs, looking out at the parkland below.
Though grainy, the photo seems to show Sylvia's face!
It's sure the tales tell it's a truly haunted place.

The Ghosts of Hotel Baker

(St. Charles, Illinois)

The title "Colonel"—an honorary appellation—
Was given Edward Baker for his fame,
Earned through amazing luck in betting
On horses. The "Colonel" had an inspiration
To build a fine hotel to keep his name.

So, it was built. But that still-elegant setting
Is said to be haunted by a pair of ghosts:
A chambermaid whose name no one recalls,
Left at the alter on her wedding day,
Drowned herself in the Fox and joined the hosts
Of spirits—lingering there (as so many times befalls)—
Seen usually on floor six dressed all in grey.

And Harriet, Baker's wife, at the witching hour,
Is sometimes seen looking down from its one tall tower.

The Ghost of Payroll Rock

(located in what is now Aurora, Illinois)

Where Turkey Creek crossed an old Indian trail
A humpbacked granite boulder marks the spot.
But the legend of that rock still makes folks quail.
The Blackhawk War—a bloody battle fought.

A place of death and carnage. Winfield Scott
Had dispatched a troop of cavalry to defend
A box of silver coins and the Paymaster.
But at that rock they met with grim disaster,
For, when the Sauk attacked, all met their end—
Down to the last man (whose name the tale forgot,
Save that he was the one they failed to save).
But, before a war-club dashed out all his brains,
He quickly dug with bare hands 'neath that rock
And hid the strongbox before he felt the shock
Of his skull cracking, his death…
                              The stone remains—
Memorial to him and the cavalrymen who gave
Their lives in the "Turkey Creek Massacre,"
As it is called.
                    But the legend says that stone
Is haunted! And on the exact day and hour,
Each anniversary of that scene of gory death,
Most strange and awful noises will occur:
They say it's the voice of one man—all alone—
Straining at heavy labor, using all his power
To finish some urgent task, gasping for breath!
Frantic to finish! But then, a scream of terror
That stops, cut short…
                        then only silence there.

Part V

Poems of Science Fiction

Springtime in Another South
(a Japanese Sonnet—invented form)

sunrise in black sky
deserts stretching far and wide
other-world morning

elliptical path
around distant yellow sun
seasons unequal

southern hemisphere
spring heads toward hot summer
wind storms, misty skies

ice cap at the pole
begins annual melting
waters trickle red
down tiny crevasses, cracks
in beds of once-great rivers

Exoplanet Reverie
(a poem in the Irish form of
Cro Cumaisc Etir Casbairdni Ocus Lethrannaigecht)

The heavens are glimmering.
This I've seen before,
But these patterns shimmering
Light an unknown shore.

Wide gulfs of space sundering
Earth, our native home,
From here, after wandering—
The vast abyss to roam.

After our long spacefaring—
Thirty light-years here!
Our pioneer race daring
To leave our blue sphere.

After the discovery—
A "goldilocks" zone
Planet! Indeed, of very
Great promise, hope shown—

Close in the infinity,
The expanse of space—
Near enough vicinity
To begin our race.

Earth dying, space beckoning,
We sailed off that day,
After one last reckoning
Of our cosmic way.

We spoke in metonymies:
"The Silence," "The Black."
None of our astronomies
Foresee going back.

* * *

The dawn! A bit frightening,
Twin suns! A strange sight.
The red dwarf glow brightening,
Driving off stark nigh

Our chromed shelter glistening
In the ruddy glow.
I am awed by listening:
Sounds I do not know!

Things in weird trees chittering
Mammal-like and small.
Above, winged things flittering;
Below—things that crawl.

The flora, not "greenery."
"Trees" and "shrubs" of brown
And red. Weird-world scenery!
…Now rain coming down.

No doubt the fertility
Of this alien soil.
Within our ability
To farm…glean with toil.

And we have surety
Both water and air
Are fine in purity,
So those aren't a care.

* * *

Our science predicated
That our crew could thrive
We must be dedicated
To prosper, to *Live!*

No one will be following
Our path to this world
Old Sol will be swallowing
As Old Earth is hurled.

We must struggle mightily
In this—our new home;
Strive to endure vitally
'Neath *"This Heaven's"* dome.

For now, it's a mystery
Just how we will fare.
We start a new history
Under red sun's glare.

Through the New Telescope

If not amazed before, we should be now.
To use a clichéd line, "It boggles the mind"
To contemplate this universal "Wow!"
Those not awed by what this scope may find
Are undeveloped souls—or else afraid
To ponder immensity, accept humility—
Seeing how huge creation has been made.
Such is beyond the too-proud mind's ability.
Unseen before—this wild, incredible vastness,
A billion billion galaxies in view!—
Amazed to see the light of primordial pastness
As now the unfathomably old is vibrant, new!
Now we should see how small a race we are,
Circling around our once-thought "central" star.

Vikings of the Void
(in an approximation of Old Norse *Ljothahattr* meter ["Song Measure"])

Vikings of the Void we venture as
Sailors of the Sea of Space.
Wormhole Warriors wandering ever
as questing Conquerors of the Cosmos.

Our longship legion firmament-leaping
crosses limitless lightyears.
We set our sails, and solar winds waft
us past novae and nebulae.

No planet's shores are proof against our prow's
grounding, greeting new galaxies.
Roving all realms, riches and rewards
our reavers reach and reap.

Navigators needing no one North Star
among the array of eons.
Mariners of the Mystery, maneuvering Space-Time,
destined to know dusks on different worlds.

So, we sail on, ever searching
the vacuous infinite vastness.
Restless, relentless, ever reaching
Pilots of the Purple Twilight.*

*The last line is directly from Alfred, Lord Tennyson's poem "Locksley Hall," from a passage that is clearly SciFi-esque:

"For I dipt into the future, far as human eye could see,
Saw the Vision of the world, and all the wonder that would be…"
Saw the heavens fill with commerce, argosies of magic sails,
Pilots of the purple twilight, dropping down with costly bales;
Heard the heavens fill with shouting, and there rain'd a ghastly dew
From the nations' airy navies grappling in the central blue;…

155

ALIEN MYSTERY:

Mysterium Aliena
Εξωγήινο Μυστήριο
[*exogíino mystírio*]

I.
Most who believe believe they come from far,
Across vast reaches of the cosmic void,
From faraway planet circling a distant star;
Perhaps come from a world that has been destroyed,
Seeking a new home on this blue-green sphere;
We hope not with hostile motive or intent,
With a technology we should rightly fear!
These wait for some definitive event.

Certain it seems there are strange things in our skies,
Beyond our capabilities or ken.
And most who question the What's, the Who's, the Why's
Believe they are beings—perhaps quite unlike men—
Who travel from the far-flung Deeps of Space,
Who will, perhaps soon, confront our human race.

II.
Yet there are some who think they come from zones—
Not spatial but dimensional! Through unknown gates
Yet unrevealed to us, from unsuspected planes
That sometimes *cross* our own. Our *Reason* abdicates
When contemplating such an argument.
Our "common sense" says "This just cannot be!"
But science assures the possibility
Of other dimensions is real. They give assent
To the theory that many others might exist
Beyond the common view there are but three.
These thinkers claim this is true, and they persist
By pointing out how frequently we see
These strange things in the sky, appearing near,
Only to somehow—as if by magic—disappear!

III.
And there are other disciples who theorize
These "visitors" are travelers through Time,
Indeed, they claim these strange craft in our skies
Are our *Future Selves!* This third great paradigm
Is no more unbelievable they say
Than the belief that beings from some distant place,
From myriad light-years across the galaxy,
Have ventured here across mind-boggling space!
And travel across *Time* is no more strange
Than thinking other *Realities* there be,
Than believing our senses must rearrange—
Allow worlds with which our senses disagree.

Whence, across Space or Dimensions they come?
Or our own selves—to view their ancient home?

Warming

[A Japanese Sonnet—invented form]

long droughts and mudslides,
flooding and vast forest fires,
hurricanes, "twisters,"

glaciers receding,
many crops drowning or baked,
polar bears dying
stranded on "ice boats,"
pestilence and stark famine
plaguing humankind.

many say it's too late—
already too late to save
our world. Sci-Fi books
speak of finding other Earths.
why not work to save this one?

Xenomnesia

(an English Sonnet in Alexandrines)

For untold ages, we have gazed up at the sky,
Amazed at the black, bejeweled, and wondrous welkin wide.
And some have sensed—most strange!—a soundless voice on high,
Not speaking words—*but thoughts!*—that would not be denied.
 "You think you are alone in all this cosmos vast;
Believe that, in this universe, you are unique?
Know you that such ideas—foolish!—cannot last.
Know that you have, at heart, the answer that you seek:
All, all are gathered from far-flung primordial dust!
All worlds congeal from multiverses widely thrown,
With multitudes of other beings—this you must
Have already surmised—nay! secretly have known."
 Such is the Deep Truth of our Alien Memory:
 Those stars share both out Past and Distant Destiny.

The Final Space Odyssey
(from the *Journal* of Under Officer, Ezekial B. Rogers, USSF)

entry: 06.29.2047
"'By the rockets' red glare,' we raced through thinning air
And soon had left the atmosphere of Earth.
It is nothing new to me—the endless blackness there
And how soon our world looks tiny in its girth.
   But the shudder that shook the ship when we
Cut rocket power and went to ion drive,
Even though we'd been prepared, was new to me.
   And the greater test is coming—to survive
The first use of our warp drive and the bubble
We will ride to find if *Trappist(dash)1e*
Is viable and will be worth our trouble
To find a place where human life can thrive.
   Of course, such Exodus is all assumption.
The plan is for us to—*in time*—return,
For many of us [*not all*] to seed resumption
Of life, so that Hope's dimming light might burn
On, since the Earth we've left is dying fast,
Days darkened by weather's whims, by nuclear blast,
By swollen seas, lost coastlines, waking volcanoes,
Enormous earthquakes…clearly the dying throes
Of a planet that has doomed itself—though warned!
Yes, warned by many…but their truths were scorned."

entry: 07.02.2047
   "I remember well the little bedtime verse
That my grandmother would every night rehearse:
'Now I lay me down to sleep,' she'd cite,
'And pray the Lord my soul to keep.' The fright
Would come—'If I should *die* before I wake,'
Not helped by 'I pray the Lord my soul to take.'
   And now I 'lay me down' for half a year,
And now it's back—the selfsame taste of Fear.
'Suspended Animation' has been tested,
But not on me! It seems like Life arrested,
But soon I'll go into that long, long sleep
We must do to survive the cosmos deep.
   At least the warp drive seems to work OK.

I'll trust the techs who say I'll wake one day.
And, if I don't, *I pray* this journal finds
Its way to some surviving human minds."
entry: 12.20.2048
   "'*I wake and feel the fell of dark, not day…*'
A couple centuries past and far away
Some fellow wrote. I feel that same way now.
The ship is dark. I'm first awake somehow.
And looking out, a different firmament
A twinkling mystery is full in view:
A myriad stars! A nebula!—all new!
   Dim, multi-colored lights of instruments
Are all that glow within that orients
My sluggish senses. Then a sight presents—
What wonder! A planet—*blue AND green!*
Through the observation window can be seen.

* * *

   My fellow crew have now begun to wake,
Cabin lights flare, as if instant daybreak
Has come. In awe, we cheer—our half-quest done—
Viewing the red star known as Trappist 1.
But more exciting, much more grand by far:
The Earth-like fifth planet rounding that red star.
   Of course, there are tests to run, the descent planned,
But it looks like Christmas will be our day to land!"

entry: 12.25.2048
   "Our tests all showed a vibrant, living globe.
Great seas (yes water!) cover a third of it…
Four great land masses…atmospheric probe
Showed oxygen aplenty! We commit
To go today. I'm in the first landing crew!
We'll touch down when all three moons are in view!
   Only ten of our twenty voyagers will descend
To land on its bright half, tidally locked,
It's like our moon with one side sunward facing.
We'll stay at least a year! But I should append
That's only about six Earth days, for it goes racing
Around its sun—quite close. And I was shocked
To learn that close red dwarf star will appear
Four times as large as Sol in that new sky!

161

Odyssey Base

We're set! We've loaded up. I've checked my gear.
We're heading down, this world to demystify!"
* * *

"What wonders! Though the atmosphere is chill—
Like the briskness of a late October day
On Earth—less gravity provides a thrill.
We all note that we actually "weigh"
Only about nine tenths of back at home.
The red sun looms so huge in this new sky!
We unfold Odyssey Base before we roam
Out from our landing craft to gratify
Our intense wonder at what lies behind
That nearby hill, covered in vegetation,
That beckons. Who knows what we'll find?
What things have sprung from *different Creation?*"
* * *

"The hill is covered in ferns with purplish fronds.
Cresting it, we see broad lands below.
Strange brownish "grasslands" and blue glittering ponds—
And Yes! They test as water! And small streams flow
To a river on the blue horizon's rim."

162

* * *

"Fauna! Among those ferns and even stranger trees!
Small things that skitter about, winged things that skim
The tree tops.
　　　　　　There, in that evernoon's chill breeze,
One stopped and looked at me with tilted head,
A wolf-sized thing, mammalian seeming, but with red,
Reptilian eyes. But then it turned away
And hurried back into the forest's gloom.
　　We searched and catalogued a full Earth Day,
We headed back to Odyssey. We'll resume
Our searches in twelve Earth hours. But we set
Defensive forcefields all about our base.
We don't have any clearcut notion yet
What dangers might be near. So, just in case,
We also set a watch. I had first turn.
**　　Two hours in, the wolf-thing came in view!**
Pacing outside the barrier, then it lay
Down on its belly, and the glowing burn
Of those red eyes, transfixed me, seemed to say:
'You are an alien thing, something quite new.'
Of course, I felt the same. It was the first
Time I'd seen how small our band of ten
Is to be braving this now not-distant world.
Shift over, I fell exhausted into my bed,
But my dreams saw watching eyes—of fiery red."

Blue

entry: 12.26.2048
"Day two of exploration. And we've found
That, thus far, no *huge* animals have appeared.
The samples from the purple ferns all around,
Should, chemically, as foodstuff, not be feared.
     We met the same wolf-thing in a forest glade,
Again, more curious than it was afraid.
I had a Spec One and Tech Sergeant cover me
As I approached the beast that I'd named "Blue"
(although its "fur" was blue of a greenish hue)
With open hand to see if it might be
Not quite as feral as was likely true.
After all, wasn't this—millennia ago—
How mankind met the wolf, made "dog" a friend?
And, without trying, just how could I know
If our two worlds could somehow start to blend?
     It shied away at first—at least no attack.
Then I threw a small lizard-thing that I'd found dead
Out toward the creature. It came slinking back.
It seemed the reptilian was quite a snack.
I told the other men that they could go.
But I knew that I had to take it slow.
I said, 'I've decided your name's Blue.'
It looked at me as if, somehow, it knew.
I planned to make more progress the next day,
Could I befriend it? Only time would say."

Several entries skipped over here. The day-to-day
search and discovery work went on. All doubts about the habit-
ability of the new world were set aside. But…
entry: 01.06.2048
"Today received: a message from the ship
We now know there's no hope of a return trip.
They found the warp drive damaged beyond repair,
Old Earth—a dream. No going back to where
Our *Odyssey* began. And we also knew
There might be no Old Earth to return to.
     The other shuttle's bringing the other ten,
And now we know we must begin again
While this our new home, perhaps, no Eden is
We must commence. Earth Two—come strife or bliss—
Is ours to build. Ten women and ten men.
This was always a hoped-against Plan B,
But now we're faced with stark reality.

We must make this world our home and multiply,
So that Earth's human species will not die.
Ah! Here's the other shuttle. There'll be another trip,
To gather and bring supplies down from the ship."

NOTE: Skipping over many entries—mostly on the discoveries, hardships, successes, and one fatality. But the colony perseveres.

entry: 7.18.2048—Journal of Ezekial-Adam, First Gen
"We're going out to hunt for food and skins
A herd of Red-Ox is only a klick away.
The doc says Sandra-Eve will be having twins,
And other Second Gens are on the way.
I must succeed for my "first cycle" bride.
And for The Colony we must provide.
How many generations now long gone
Have brought us here? But we few must move on.
We cannot rest. Our task—*one poet read*—
In a hologram that stuck into my head:
'To strive, to seek, to find, and not to yield.'
* * *
Ah! here are the Red-Ox, strewn across the field.
Our hunt will be true. We will not be denied.
Our prey awaits—and Blue is by my side.

165

A Terraformer's Lament

We found this planet worthy of terraforming
Only a century past, and now we're near
Completion of the work, the *Natural* "norming."
We have *Earth Two* complete, and yet I fear
The things that plagued us on our now-dead Earth
Have followed us, been with us all along.
We sought a bright start, a new Edenic birth:
Clean air, calm climate, a balance—but we were wrong.
We, we *underlings* have not broken free
From our *human nature*—always our true curse—
From, not Eve's and Adam's, but our family tree.
Transplanted Evils, now bad are growing worse.
Though Hope still lives, perhaps the fate of Man
Is to defy, defile all Good we can.

PART VII

POLITICAL POEMS

THIS SECTION KILLS FASCISTS

A New Crisis

As happens with the rolling Wheel of Years,
Epochs of conflict and relative calm will roll
On and ever on. Hopes vie with Fears.
Ever and always Ignorance takes its toll.
Again comes round a Time when every soul
Is tried—at least those not mired in Apathy,
Blinded by Prejudice or Demagoguery.
A time again to write upon the Scroll
Of History—again with a Righteous Hand.
Again, we may cry "Peace, Peace!" but there is none.
Once more the Time has come to save Our Land,
Else our great Founding Principles are undone.
Ballots, not bullets for this next Revolution,
That the Rules of Law and Justice ever stand.

America the …?

O dutiful, the MAGAt mind,
A hive of deaf, blind bees,
Who more than our land a despot love
Who would bring to its knees
America! America?!
God bestow sense on thee!
Revive, once good—our Nationhood,
Else we shall not be free.

Once beautiful our patriot dream
That sought throughout the years,
To make us better than we seem—
A nation fraught with fears.
America! America!
God mend thine every flaw.
Confirm thy soul, regain control
Through righteous Truth and Law!

Absolute Power and The Gates of Hell

The quote rephrased: "Absolute Corruption
Results from Power Absolute." It seems
That this holds true, Reason's abruption
Is all too common in "Social" Media streams.
No doubt our "Founding Fathers' were too heedful
Not to extend our Freedoms' scant restraints
For now, quite clearly, what is fully needful
Are limits to Hate Speech, Death threats—all that taints
The all-too-common uncommonly deformed souls,
Whose spewing out of lies and vitriol
Threaten ideals of peace and love for all,
Rational democracy—all of our greatest goals.
When demagogues and filthy rich hold sway,
Each new dawn ushers in a darker day.

A Sad Misnomer

The term "brainwashing" is sadly incorrect.
Its denotation: the brain is somehow *cleaned!*
In truth, it takes advantage of defect;
Its purpose: the power of Reason shall be weaned
From a mind and soul already unevolved,
Not strong enough in rationality
To weigh disparate "Facts," to remain absolved
From sorting wheat from chaff with acuity.

And sadder still, those subject to such "cleaning,"
Once "cleansed," are adamant in each belief
Accepted as "Truth." And lies, devoid of any meaning,
Perpetuate and spread. Thus, general woe and grief
Are brought upon us through these "ill-washed" brains.
Perhaps, full soon, we'll find what Truth remains.

Damnatio Memoriae

Let his name be condemned, but never forgotten.
Perhaps remove all graven words of praise,
All images that show a smiling lie.
But, like the Holocaust, abysmal, rotten,
Reviled be his memory—he who would raise
Rebellion in our land, who would deny
Our basic principles of free democracy
For personal power and gain, who would supplant
The essential, underlying power of the vote,
Replace it with a foul autocracy.
Let cordial debate replace a tyrant's rant;
Let his legacy be the darkest, grim footnote:
A blot that Time may hopefully erase,
At least diminish—past this great disgrace.

Proditor Dux

(after Shelly's "Ozymandias")
[The far-distant future: A.D. 3024]

A traveler from a distant planet stood
And looked at an effigy obliterated on the ground.
  "This broken figure once—in all likelihood
(Telepathically, of course. It made no sound
Communicating with its fellow pioneers
Who'd crossed the endless vastness of deep space)—
Was a being who once held power in this barren place,
But clearly who earned great infamy through the years.
  "The evidence is here in these many scattered
Shards, these fragments of a statue of strange stone.
Such damage could not have come from long years alone.
No doubt this simulacrum's form was shattered
By forceful blows. And see—the statue's base too is defaced
These long-dead words must tell of one disgraced."

'Semper falsa verba eius.
Se supra rempublicam amaverat.'

['His words were always false.
He loved himself above the Republic.']

In Propaganda Terms, It's Called "Transfer"
[upon the "president" watching a display of military might]

Surrounded by so much red and white and blue,
Subconsciously, to some it might seem true
That weakness, lacking principles is right
When juxtaposed beside a nation's might.
Meanwhile, ignoring all the righteous rage
'Gainst humans kept within a crowded cage,
Against the friendly face shown enemies,
While old friendships are shaken by unease.
There were some "teaching moments" in this whim—
Now people know the Coast Guard has a hymn.
Who didn't know already our nation's might,
Was meant to defend the Rule of Law and Right,
And fight against the forces of Evil's Night?
    Center stage, the Master of the Ceremony,
Put on a sober face, spewed out baloney,
In yet another speech—not by THIS phony,
By some team hired to *eloquize* his speech,
So there would be no gross, horrendous breach
Of language or of thought—or Reason's Laws.
Avoiding all of his ad-libbing flaws.
    Symbolic with each branch's airpower pass,
The "Chief" would turn and watch and show his ass.
Safely behind the bulletproof panes of glass.
And what did this show do to our holiday,
Time—as it will—will pass. And who can say?
Red Hats abounding in the human sea,
Filled in the dearth when he took the presidency.
But, on our flag, Red is but one bold hue:
The Blue is for Union—though sorely tried—still True.
White's Dream of Peace most hope for me and you.
Let's stop the excess Red that's bleeding through.

Will We Keep It? [1]

Outside Independence Hall after the Constitutional Convention in 1787—
unidentified woman: "Doctor, what have we got? A republic or a monarchy?"
Franklin: "A republic, if you can keep it."
—from the notes of Dr. James McHenry, one of
Maryland's delegates to the Convention.

The question still resounds: "What have we got?"
The worst division since a Civil War
Now plagues our land. And we are caught
Between a Dark Dilemma's Horns once more.
A lack of Reason plagues too large a faction
Equivocators claim that Truths are "Fake".
When clear and present lies are told, reaction
Divides the Echo-Chambered and Awake.
A would-be despot, autocrat, and egotist,
Bemired in scandals, guilty of traitorous acts,
Spews on "the Big Lie," continues to enlist
An ignorant mass unmoved by glaring Facts.
Can we, at this grave moment, keep a Republic whole
And somehow hold onto our Nation's Soul?

Will We Keep It? [2]

"Well, Doctor, what kind of government do we have?"
Or something to that effect, the lady* asked.
To which Ben Franklin allegedly replied:
"A republic—if you can keep it." Can we save
That dream of governance? We have been tasked
To do so. And it might be said we've tried.

But clearly—within two-hundred-fifty years—
We have lost touch with the essence of that plan;
That strong "center" has not held; the Eagle flies
Near to beyond a Dread Horizon. Fears
Of the dissolution of that Dream that began
In "brotherly love"** are now brought on by lies.

And those who should represent the public weal,
Leave unattended wounds that may not heal.

*According to the likely best account of Franklin's legendary statement regarding
the "kind of government" that we have, the journal of James McHenry, a delegate
to the Constitutional Convention from Maryland, the question was asked by
Mrs. Elizabeth Willing Powell, a Philadelphia socialite.

** Philadelphia derives its name from the Greek, "phileo" (to love) and "adelphos"
(brother): hence, its moniker as "The City of Brotherly Love."

Plague Fatigue: London 1349
[Proof that History doesn't "repeat itself," but—
as Mark Twain noted: "…it often rhymes."
Ignorance can be cured. Stupidity can't.]

"Here comes that bloomin' cart again.
Fie on that curséd shout!
This plague has become such a pain.
'Hey Yo! Bring your dead out!'"
"But, Husband Dear, I greatly fear
This plague is here to stay.
It's been now more than a year
Since we, for fear, might stray."
"Well, Wife, the children yearn for fun,
And I share in their pain.
I swear, before tomorrow's sun,
I'll have my old life again!"
"But what shall the children and I do
When you are gone away?"
"Keep well your customed huswifery,
And they with our rats can play.
Enough of this boring quarantine!
Enough of this 'stay home' shite!
I do not fear what can't be seen;
I'll be at the pub tonight!
"I think this whole thing is a hoax.
The nobles do as they please,
While we're the brunt of all their jokes,
And beset by rats and fleas!
"No, no—I'll have my revelry
They call this 'The Black Death'
Merely to frighten you and me—
Beer and cheer 'fore my last breath!"

Part VII

Ekphrastic, Metapoetic, Light, and more Traditional Verses

Considering Fuseli's "The Nightmare"

"…a mara, [is] a spirit that, in heathen mythology, was related to torment or to suffocate sleepers. A morbid oppression in the night resembling the pressure of weight upon the breast."
—Samuel Johnson's *A Dictionary of the English Language* (1755)

With death-pale eyes, the *Horse* is shadowed there.
But something worse! A *Thing* of hideous shape
Sits—hulking—atop a fainted damsel fair.
Fainted? or Dead!
               A face like a fiendish ape
Turns to us, chiaroscuroed against the pale
Complexion of the girl, whose snow-white gown—
Is stark against the black that does not fail:
Background of Gloom. Her arms and head hang down.

Is this an *incubus*, a demon of night,
Come forth to violate a woman pure?
Or *mara*, a dread suffocating wight
Who sits upon the breast 'til death is sure?

Shelley and Poe viewed this work—and they knew
That Art can bring True Horrors into view.

Considering Murnau's *Nosferatu*

By flickering light, a silhouette mounts the stairs.
We scream in silence! Yet we cannot turn away.
The movie's magic captures us unawares,
Transports us far—and to a long-gone day.
A *Shadow* only, mounting to her room,
But we've met Count Orlof, know his heinous shape
Gaunt, bald, and bat-eared, centered fangs of doom,
Deep in our fears, we know there's no escape.

Claw-fingered, shadow hand moves toward her door;
Umbrageous digits clasp the victim's heart;
The monster feeds!
                  But then comes the bright sunrise.
The vampire disappears! A smoke puff from the floor
Rises—A clever effect of Silent Era art.
But help has come too late! She sighs and dies.

Considering Munch's "The Scream"

'Neath blood-red sky, a river darkly blue.
The bridge is there; we know not where from, where to.
Out of the frame, we cannot see its span.
We focus upon the ghostly screaming man.
A figure fittingly dressed all in black,
Two strange black figures follow at his back.
Under the orange-red welkin the river flows—
To? From? the black and distant hills—Who knows?
The sharp, dissecting angle of the bridge's rail
Make *Still Life* stir. His cry can never fail!
Who are those two who follow in his trail?
His hands clapped to his ears? Stifling his wail?
Pendent between weird sky and unreal land,
Is his a scream we all may understand?

The Weird Sisters: Macbeth's Witches

Those three, by light of Hecate's crescent moon,
Foredoomed Macbeth with cursed, prophetic spells.
Their conjurings, their cauldron, their words an evil rune
Sent from the regions of the deepest Hells.
The frailties of a man who would be king,
Spurred on by a woman lusting for queenly power,
Made treacherous murder seem the natural thing—
At first. But then the deed would fester and devour
Them both. Those sisters weird can be compared
To pagan goddesses, the very Fates:
Clotho, Lachesis, Atropos. The *Moirai* spared
None. Spinning, Measuring, Cutting—the tale relates.
Weird sisters, witches who befouled Life's thread—
Leaving bloodstained Macbeth and his Lady dead.

The Cat Comes on Little Fog Feet
(with a nod to Sandburg)

The cat comes on little fog feet.
It sits, silent on its furry haunches.
Most fastidious, supremely neat,
It calmly grooms itself, then naps, or launches
Itself across the floor, out the doorway—
A "morning crazy" or just a whim
Or, just perhaps, it's found one more way
To be itself, show off its vim.
True to kind, an independent cuss,
Evolving distinct habits all its own,
A unique soul, each autonomous puss
Establishes its realm and knows its throne.
   And yet, its spirit, even so defined,
   Deigns to befriend us—we poor humankind.

Po-here-tics
(a Neo-Neo-Classical Complaint
—with a nod to Pope)

Too much free verse, that has been "all the rage,"
Is merely prose placed oddly on the page.
And "prose poems" claiming to be fraught with message,
Are, all too often, prose in purple passage.
These "freer forms" delight in breaking rules,
Eschewing all time-honored versing schools,
Pretending so-called "organic" line variety
Is inspired— not mere illusion of spontaneity.

Most would-be poets of "traditional verse"
Stock lines and worn-out chimes they will rehearse.
And, even if they grasp good use of rhyme,
They prove they have no sense of keeping time.

Great poems—or free or formal wrought—"will out!"
Poor poems are more than plenty. There's no doubt.

A Futile Quest

(an *Interlocking Ballade Royal Supreme*—an invented form)

Some writers would explore the *Depths of Horror*,
Searching the *Genre* across its sub-types vast.
Through stories hoar, gore-laden, they will pour,
Delving *Domains of Darkness* do they dast,
Seeking for *Secrets* that the long-dead past
Mought keep....Could one but find *a Hidden Key!*
Some would be willing to pay any fee!

"Mayhap," they think, "I'll find a *Spell* to cast
Upon the page to set *True Terror* free;
To *scribe* the lines of *Abject Fear* that last
Long past the *Singing Pen* none can foresee;
To sail beyond the *Horizon of Horror's Sea,*
Discover grim things there and bring them home!"
But none have that far ventured—though they roam.

The Goal: To capture in a *Terror Tome*
The words that chill the marrow of the bone,
The precise phrasings in stark prose or poem,
Which, once are read, take readers to *That Zone,*
Where winds wail wild with weirding tone,
Where none, thus far, have traveled. Where few want
To go. The words that would forever *Haunt.*

Nor to that *Realm* has *any Artist* gone:
Though painters, musicians, sculptors vaunt
Some works, though clearly brilliant, none
Have reached the *Summum Terrorem.* None can flaunt
The emotional *Depths of Fear* that *all Arts* daunt.
Though *We, as Writers,* have tried various
Modes and *Means*—all are precarious.

Though powerful words and works mysterious
Voyage close in verbiage to *Horror's Darkest Shore,*
The problem is: though *Terrors* vicarious
To great degree may make the reader *Feel,*
They but evoke a *Shadow*—a *Seeming of the Real.*
TRUE*Verbal Terror* is illusory at the core.
Yet writers still explore the *Depths of Horror.*

"Stained" Glass/"Strained" Words

"I act as the tongue of you…tied in your mouth,
in mine it begins to be loosened"
—Whitman
(a double sonnet)

The artist who selects color, size, and shape
To form the wonders that we name "stained" glass
Can be likened to the poet, who must escape
From the near infinitude of words, the daunting mass
Of verbal possibilities a language holds.
   The lead used to assemble those glass bits
Into a marvel through which *True Light's* rays
Transluce the artist's vision and remolds
Our own is like *the molten line* that fits
So rightly in the well-wrought poem that says
Just what the receiver thought or felt but could
"Not quite put into words."
               The connotation
Of *"Stained"* is negative—but the result is grand.
   In that same negative sense "Strain" is often taken,
But *at least two meanings thereof* we understand:
   With one—*the discovered words*—true poets "sift"
Through *sieves of mind and soul,* with agitation,
Until fine "ore" is found—as with gold panned.
   With the other, by intense effort through one's gift,
From some deep muses' well, on the sure foundation
Of the *developed soul*—through all Life has betided,
Through all one's learning, through serendipities,
Through all that Nature and Nurture have provided—
Flow lines well-wrought, *well-"worked,"* well-planned.
Mayhap a work *strains* forth that can well please,
Enthrall, inspire, amaze deeply mind or heart.
   True Artists *strain* through their vari-*stainèd* days
Before departing—to leave behind True Art.

An Ultra-Aging of Shakespeare's "Sonnet 18"
In a "guesstimation" of Proto-Indo-Europen AND
of one hypothetical Proto-Sapeins/Proto-World Syntax.

I thee a summer's day to shall compare?
Thou more lovely and more temperate art?
Rough winds the darling buds May of do shake,
And lease summer of all too short a date hath.
The eye heaven of sometimes too hot shines,
And gold complexion his often is dimmed;
And every fair fair from sometime declines,
Chance by, or changing course nature of, untrimmed.

But eternal summer thy fade not shall,
Nor possession that fair thou ow'st of lose;
Nor Death thou shade his in wander'st shall brag
When thou eternal lines in time to grow'st;
Men so long as can breathe or eye can see,
This so long lives, and this life thee to gives.

1. The likely syntax of these ancient and long-dead languages was SOV
    (Subject-Object-Verb).
2. Adjectives precede the words they modify.
3. Prepositions are actually "Postpositions," following the phrases to which
    they relate.
4. Possessors follow that which is possessed "book John [of]" (in keeping
    with # 3) rather than "John's book").

"Proto-World" or the theory of a single original human language, parent of all
the world's language is greatly debated (and, of course, pretty much impossible
to prove). Scholars such as Merritt Reulen, and other have proposed its existence
and worked to show relationships among the world's language families.

Octothorpy

(with apologies to Dylan Thomas
and Lewis Carroll—Well, not really. I hope they'd enjoy it)

KeyboardWise by shift key at his Macintosh,
the English prof lay sleepward in his queries.
The ampersand with a taste for asterisk
bit out the "at sign" with a jaw for circumflex
and Mimsy chortled around with greenish fairies.
* * *

Beware the Octothorpe, My Child
Its tic-tack toes, the lines that snatch ye.
Beware the Dollar Sign and hum
A frabjous tune that's hip and classy.

He took his verbal sword in hand,
Long time the fee fi foe he sought.
Then rested he by the re-turn key
And sat a nonce in thought.

Then, as in shift-keyed case he stood,
The Octothorpe with tags of hash
Came signing numbers through the wood
And twittered, "Balderdash!"

One, two! Three, four! And chop and chop
The verbal blade did no line spare.
The Octothorpe with limbs beshorn
Was left dead—as a Square!

"And hast thou slain the Octothorpe!
Hie thee hither to my upper appendages thou squeamish kid!
As the Irish say: 'Harroo, Harray!'
We all ken what you did."

And thus, the Octothorpe was stopped,
That Number Sign, that Hash Tag fey.
All its eight "legs" were garkly chopped—
But they all grew back next day!

188

The Apprentice Mage Has Questions

"Why can't I look into the Sun and not be blinded,"
Young Unlaird asked of Witega, his Master and Great Mage.
    "Thou'st asked this once before, need'st thou be reminded?"
The old man frowned, then turned another vellum page
Of the ancient tome writ in a strange tongue lost to most.
But then he paused and turned to his young acolyte:
    "Thou know'st thy power of vision would be the bitter cost.
Think of it this way, boy, the Sun is our world's Painter.
All colors and shades you see, though dark or brilliant bright,
All shapes and forms, whether clear and distinct or fainter,
Are from His brush strokes, his dabbling for our view.
    "And we must appreciate these sights we have been given,
We may imitate this creation, but nothing truly new
Can come from our powers, far less than those of Heaven.
    "It is enough the Sun gives to us warmth and light.
Enough to see the Painting; the Painter's Face is not our right."

About Time

(sonnets in the Spanish form of Verso Pareado—invented form)

Continuum

The common belief that's held by almost all:
Time's linearity has us all in thrall.
We live the Present moment—ever passing;
The Past is a great monument amassing;
The Future we may predict but is unknown.
Each Moment arrives and then has swiftly flown
To trail in our Vessel's Wake as we sail on,
Ahead through each day's sunset, through next day's dawn—
Ahead through the Grey of Gloaming, Dark of Night,
Expecting that soon will come the Morning's Light.

This Truth we near universally avow:
We float on Time's River of the Here and Now
With memories and thoughts of There and Then,
All moving toward the final Where and When.

Simultaneity

But some will contend that *What Will Be* is done,
That *All That Has Passed* is warmed by This Day's sun,
That even *Here and There exist Everywhere.*
Our Sense of Time is Illusion they declare.
A Simultaneous *Parallelity,*
Beyond the comprehension of you and me
Is the Reality we refuse to hold.
And nothing is truly New or truly Old.
Throw out your belief in an effect, a cause,
Since What Will Be is also What Is, What Was.
All Ticks of Time, All Places are Now and Here.
Thus, belief in Time's Linear Flow is Mere
Mirage they tell us—easy to act aloof.
Still, most all deny this for the lack of proof.

The Coming of Autumn
(a Balanced Sonnet)

A first chill breeze has come, assaults my cheek!
Now nears the season of the waning year.
No holding summer fast, though we might seek
To do so. Soon come grey days and cool nights drear.
Soon winter's blasts with deadly cold shall maim
The land, the trees. The trees' green wings will sere.
Yet autumn leaves, though dying, fill with flame.

Such is it always as the seasons wheel,
Transform us through the stations of the sun.
All weathers, whether foul or fair we feel—
And feeling means our race is not quite run.
So, I will welcome this Fall's swift advance
And all Falls—'til the great, good trek is done,
And my time joins with *All Time's* great expanse.

Calliope
(a poem in Trisengrafs, invented FORM for vers libre)

I

I suspect that even Homer knew
    that you were not real, but, even if you were,
        he'd have to do the heavy work himself.

That, smith-like, like Hephaestus' smarter brother,
    he'd have to hammer out the hexameters
        in the fire and forge of his own mind.

The epithets and stock lines helped, of course,
    with the "wine dark sea," "Cloud Gatherer"—
        "Hector, Tamer of Horses," but the rest of the MUSE-ic...

II

THAT came from the deep understanding he had
    of his fellow mortals and the human heart,
        beating in dactyls and spontaneous spondees.

No, you were not needed—
    neither then nor now—
        the obligatory "Invocation" was just that:

Perfunctory opening so he could get on with it.
    Without a "divine afflatus" for a prompt,
        he simply took in a breath—and began.

The Road Stretches On
(based upon the rhythms of "All the Road Runnin"
by Mark Knopfler)

The road stretches on from where it began,
Far back along the trail.
I'm weary from the walking,
But I cannot afford to fail.
The way is rocky, and the path is not wide;
Many obstacles get in the way.
But I'll push ever onward,
And I will reach road's end one day.

The broad sky above, the grand lands below,
They ease the long trek's pain.
I pause at some hard places,
But then back to the journey again.
I've learned well the lesson; there are struggles ahead,
But the struggles will go to the strong.
And I will strive on undaunted,
Singing my vagabond song.

How many the travelers have led the way,
Along this selfsame trail?
All weary from the walking,
Who had hoped they would never fail?
Ah! there up ahead is my journey's end.
I'll press on with my will and a prayer.
These last long miles I'll travel.
I will find what's waiting there.

To An Athlete Dying Old

(a response to Housman)

The honors faded—oh so long ago.
Dim echoes of the cheering crowds are gone.
And here you sit, much nearer dusk than dawn.
Most of the comrades passed, those who would know
And honor long the skills you once would show.
Still, from the depths of Memory are drawn
Those deep-past days. In mind, once more you don
The uniform to battle the friendly foe.

Your records, long eclipsed yet still recorded,
Were never destined to survive for aye.
Though tarnished are the medals once awarded,
And far in the past the tests you lived to vie,
None can say truly your life was unrewarded.
And there are far less noble ways to die.

When All Is Said and Done

"When all is said and done…" a frightful clause,
Fraught with finality. It's the "*All*" that shocks.
Old Time ticks on, relentless, without pause,
As its seeming endless flow rolls on and rocks
Us into pondering those clichéd words.
What happens *Then*, when all is done and said?
Will it be as if a sounding flight of birds
Of a sudden disappear or drop down dead?
Or, more apocalyptic, with a super-nova-ed sun,
Have nothing left to drop to. Our blue-green orb
Turned cosmic dust—*when all is said and done.*
All *endings* are mysteries veiled, thorny to absorb.
  Yet there are things never said nor written—bravely new—
  And deeds both grand and righteous we might yet do.

Poem on My Birthday
(29 June 2023)

Beyond the primroses of April and May
The summer roses of June will stay.
Loveliest of flowers, the roses blow
In my birth month—as long ago—
'Cross many lands in many a garden.
And I have one more year of pardon!

Though dormant under winter's snow,
The time swings 'round, and again they grow;
And I comfort when, in our Northern freeze,
They glory in the antipodes.

Hours, days, weeks, months, and seasons swift
Fly by. But each new year's a gift.

Now of my "ten years and three score"
I've been allowed a few odd more.
And here I stand at seventy-five:
A milestone—*not millstone*—haply alive.
Twenty-five "leagues" of distance run—
Well past when this great race was begun.

And though it seems each coming June
Apace approaches…much too soon,
Recalling the wise words, "Getting older
Is better than not," makes my heart bolder.
Of this long road there's much behind,
But the road ahead is in my mind.
I know the Truth in heart and soul:
The journey's as great as is the goal,
And the path ahead—where'er I roam—
Is part of the grand *returning home.*

Glossary of Forms

(Definitions and Explanations
of the many and various
cross-cultural, cross-epochal,
and invented forms
used in this book)

Ae Freslige and Ae Freslige Sonnet (invented form):
The Irish quatrain, *Ae Freslige*, is comprised of heptasyllabic lines, making use of an ABAB rhyme scheme and alternating triple and double end-rhymes. Thus, 7(3)-7(2)-7(3)-7(2). To create the Ae Freslige Sonnet, I have added a couplet of 7-syllable lines with double rhymes (although the final couplet could be on triple rhymes, alternatively). NOTE: A poem thus formed has the same rhyme pattern as the English/Shakespearean Sonnet—although distinctive due to the highly restrictive rhyming pattern and syllabic rather than accentual-syllabic measure.

Aicill Rhyme:
Aicill rhyming is a common technique in ancient Irish verse. Essentially, the last syllable of one line rhymes with either the first or an internal syllable of the next.

Alcmanics / Alcmanic Sonnet (invented form):
Used by the poet Alcman of Sparta (fl. 7th c. B.C.). His verses varied from the more common dactylic hexameter (as in Homer's epics) by using hypercatalectic dactylic tetrameter lines, approximated in accentual/syllabic meter by /uu /uu /uu / in ten syllables. Fourteen lines in this meter form the Alcmanic Sonnet.

Asclepiadean Meter / Asclepiadean Sonnet (invented form) and Choriambics in general:
Asclepiades of Samos (born. c. 320 B.C.) made use of the metrical foot of the choriamb(us) [/uu/], a foot of four syllables, approximeted in accentual/syllabic poetry in two forms:
The Lesser Asclepiad (a line of 12 syllables[dodecasyllabic])
[two anapests, a choriamb(us), an iamb(us)]
uu/uu/ * /uu/u/
The Greater Asclepiad (a line of 16 syllables [hexadecasyllabic])
(two anapests, two choriambs, an iamb(us): uu/ uu/ /uu/ /uu/ u/
My **Asclepiadean Sonnet** uses the Lesser Aesclepiad as a base, although the longer line of the Greater Aesclepiad might be used.

Balassi Stanza and Balazzi Stanza Sonnet:
The Balassi Stanza was the inspiration for my conversion of the form into a sonnet. It is attributed to Bálint Balassi (1554-1594) who is probably Hungary's best known Renaissance poet. He transformed it from a three-line form consisting of 19-syllable lines with internal rhymes into three-line groups of 6-6-and 7 syllables, with the six-syllable lines ending with what would be

the "internal" rhyme of the long 19-syllable version and the seven-syllable line carrying the main rhyme, thus: AABCCBDDB for a nonain or nonastich stanza or poem.

I have reverted a bit toward the older form in my Ballassi Stanza Sonnet* by using divisions of 12-7 and providing the internal rhymes in the twelve-syllable lines with the rhyme on syllables 6 and 12. Thus, the expansion of Balassi's pattern into an octave of 12-7-12-7-12-7-12-7 with the shorter lines carrying the main rhyme, followed by a sestet of 12-7-12-7-12-7—again with the internal rhymes different and the shorter lines carrying the main rhyme, *but also on a different rhyme from the octave.*

Ballade Royal and Ballade Royal Supreme (the latter, an invented form):
The Ballade Royale differs from the regular Ballade in that it uses the Rhyme Royal stanza (used by Geoffrey Chaucer and others). This stanza rhymes ABABBCC. The last line of the first stanza is repeated as a refrain in succeeding stanzas. There can be any number of succeeding stanzas, and the Ballade Royale differs from the standard Ballade in that it does not use a differently rhymed envoi, but finishes the poem with a final Ryme Royal stanza. My transformation of this to the Ballade Royal Supreme has either "Open" or "Interlockiing" forms. The Open Ballade Royal Supreme uses, as is, perhaps, suggested by the title, a simple sequence of diffferently rhymed Rhyme Royal stanzas with no need to repeat the As, Bs, and Cs of the first stanza. The "Interlocked" Form is a bit more restrictive, demanding echoes from one stanza to the next. As follows:
Ababbcc
bdbddee
dfdffgg
fhfhhii
. . . . etc,
hjhjjaA
And with A being a refrain of the first line of the poem.

Ballade Supreme a Double Refrain:
The Ballade Supreme a Double Refrain is an isosyllabic poem (a poem with lines of a fixed syllable count, but of the same count in every line) of 35 lines divided into three ten line sections and a five-line envoi.
Each line is usually eight or ten syllables long. It has two refrains lines
The rhyming and repeats are: ababbCcdcD for three sections, with the envoi rhyming cCdcD. C and D are the refrain lines.

Balanced Sonnet:
(a "Balanced Sonnet"" is a scheme invented by Barbara Dilworth (what she also
called "The California Rhyme Scheme)": ABABCBC DEDEFDF.

Breton Sonnet (invented form):
While my version of a "Breton Sonnet" fits the rhyme patterns and syllable
count lengths of Breton poetry (either couplets or AABCCB in normally
octasyllabic or dodecasyllabic lines), it does not use the normal *Kenganez*
[harmony] parallel to Welsh *Cynghanedd*. In true *kenganez*, either two or
three internal rhymes are common AND the penultimate syllable of each line
must rhyme with the internal rhymes of the line AND the end-rhymes of
the AA and CC lines need to cross-rhyme into the B lines, respectively. This,
believe me, is damned near impossible in English for any sustained number
of stanzas I have created the "Breton Sonnet" by adding a couplet to the two
hexains to make fourteen lines. The rhyme scheme of AABCCB DDEFFE
leads into the final couplet.

Burmese Ya-Du:
The Ya-Du is a Burmese poetic form. Here are the guidelines of this
intricate form: 1) written in quuintains/pentastiches (five-line stanzas);
2) 4 syllables in the first four lines; 3) the final line has either 5, 7, 9, or
11 syllables; 4) the fourth syllable of the first line rhymes with the third
syllable of the second line and the second syllable of the third line' 5)
The fourth syllable of the third line rhymes with the third syllable of the
fourth line and the second syllable of the fifth line' 6) the fourth syllable
of the fourth line rhymes with the final syllable of the final line' 7) the
subject usually deals with seasons.
   Most ya-du are written in three or fewer stanzas.

Catena Rondo:
The Catena Rondo is a form invented by Canadian poet Robin Skelt-
on in his seminal book on poetic forms, *The Shapes of Our Singing*. He
took the name from *catena*, which means "chain" and *rondo*, which means
"round" or "circle." The poem features a great many repeated lines.
The rules for the Catena Rondo: 1) yhe poem is comprised of any num-
ber of quatrains' 2) each quatrain has a rhyme pattern of AbbA; 3) the
first line of each quatrain is repeated as the final line of the quatrain; 4)
the second line of each quatrain is the first line of the next quatrain; 5)
the final quatrain should repeat the first quatrain word for word,
There are no rules for meter, syllables, or subject matter.

Cauderna Via / Cauderna Via Sonnet (invented form):
*Cuaderna Via ["the four-fold way] is a medieval Spanish form done in 14-syl-
lable, mono-rhymed quatrains, with the rhymes having consonance as well (in
other words, comprised of no vocalic or "vowel only" rhymes). I have truncated
the final group to two lines to make fourteen for this inventedsonnet. Ideally,
in the form, the fourteen-syllables that make up the lines are two 7-syllable
hemistiches or "half-lines, commonly separated by a caesura.

Clogyrnach and the Clogyrnach Sonnet (invented form):
A Clogyrnach begins with an eight-syllable couplet, followed by lines of
five, five, three, and three syllables. The three-three pair may be, and often
is, written as one six-syllable line. The five syllable lines rhyme with each
other and with the first of the threes; the second three rhymes with the
original couplet. So the syllable pattern is 8-8-5-5-3-3 (or 8-8-5-5-6).

For the Clogyrnach Sonnet (VI "Moons of Doom" p. 7), I truncated
the last section to make four lines to make the total 14, as required by the
sonnet form.

I've taken some liberties with the counts in the final quatrain is 8-6-6-
7 with envelope rhyme and cross-rhyme from the penultimate line into
the final line of the poem.

Cornish Sonnet:
Some theorize that the Cornish Sonnet was influenced by Arab traders
to the Cornish coast. It is comprised of two hexains, each consisting of
an enclosed tercet (axa), but with the central line of the tercets rhyming.
Thus, Abacbc Dedfef. As indicated by the capitals in this rhyme scheme,
The lines A and D are repeated as refrains, appearing in the two-line con-
clusion to this quatorzain. So: Abacbc Dedfef AD. The meter can be any
variety or line length of the poet's choosing—although usually syllabic.

Cornish "Type II" Sonnet (invented form):
According to scholar Benjamin Bruch, the Cornish Type II Stanza is a
hexain rhyming AABCCB. The lines are usually heptasyllabic, and one
finds either the first or both of the B-rhymed lines at four syllables. I have
two rhyming lines to the octave in Sonnet XXVI to make a fourteener.

Cross-Rhyme:
Many of the Celtic forms (Welsh, Irish, Cornish, etc.) make use of cross-
rhyme. As the name suggests, a syllable at the end of one line rhymes into
the beginning or middle of the next. Some Welsh forms also double this
by having a medial syllable of a line becoming the ending sound of the

Cross Rhyme (cont.)
next, and the final sound of the first line rhyming into the beginning or middle of the next.

Cro Cumaisc Etir Casbairdni Ocus Lethrannaigecht:
How's THAT for a long Irish name?. Robin Skelton, in his important book, *The Shapes of Our Singing*, explains this form as syllabic quatrains of 7-5-7-5 syllables with the 7-syllable lines ending in triple rhymes and the 5-syllable lines ending in single rhymes and usually on single-syllable words. The rhyme scheme is ABAB. The third line may sometimes end in a disyllabic word, in which case it rhyme into the middle of the following line (see **Aicil Rhyme**).

"Curtal English Sonnet" (invented form):
Just as Gerard Manley Hopkins created his "Curtal Sonnet" by doing a mathmatical reduction of the 8:6 division ratio of the Italian/Petrarchan sonnet, coming up with a form of 6 lines followed by 4 1/2 lines. I have reduced the English/Shakespearean Sonnet from its base of three quatrains and a couplet (4-4-4-2) to a poem of 3-3-3-1 1/2 lines. Sonnet LVIII, "Now is the Bright Nighttime" (p. 70) also makes use of terza rima, rhyming ABA BCB CDC Dd. NOTE: These tercets could be triplets, OR could be repeated [ABC ABC ABC], OR be unrhymed— OR rhymed in any other fashion to also qualify as a "Curtal English Sonnet." The distinction is in the divisions of the poem and the half line at the end. Yes, not technically a "sonnet," but definitely "curtal" or "curtailed" in the mode Hopkins used.

Cyhydedd Naw Ban / Cyhydedd Naw Ban Sonnet (invented form):
Cyhydedd Naw Ban (*ki-hi-deth now bahn*) is a Welsh official meter using 9-syllable lines in rhymed couplets. The use of any or some or all of the "Harmonies" / Cynghanedd is optional, but frequent. Seven of these couplets make up the **Cyhydedd Naw Ban Sonnet.**

Dechnad Mor / Dechnad Mor Sonnet (invented form):
As with almost all Celtic meters and forms, Dechnad Mor is very difficult to produce in English.

The basic pattern of this Irish form is in syllabic quatrains of 8(2) 6(2) 8(2) 6(2) [where the 8 6 8 6 indicate the total syllable counts of the lines and the 2s in parentheses indicate that the rhymes must be on two syllables—in other words, double rhymes.

The rhyme scheme of each quatrain is ABAB. Note further that these

echoes can be merely consonances rather than full rhymes.
Ideally, every line has alliteration on at least two syllables.

The end word of lines 1 and 3 should, ideally, rhyme, assonate, or consonate with a syllable in the beginning of lines 2 and 4, respectively. This is a form of *Aicill Rhyme*. This last pattern has been very loosely followed in this poem.

I have added an octosyllabic double-rhymed couplet to three Dechnad Mor quatrains to complete the fourteen lines of a sonnet.

Decima Italiana:
The Décima Italiana is: 1) stanzaic, written in any number of 10 line stanzas; 2) syllabic, 8 syllables per line, or in Italianate lines (mixed or irregular 11 and 7 syllable lines); 3) rhymed, ABABC DEDEC; 4) ,the Crhyme must be masculine rhyme [the rhyming syllable must be accented]; 5) L5 must be end stopped.

Dizain:
The dizain is aFrench form. This particular form was a favorite of 15th and 16th century French poets, but it has also been employed in English by the likes of Philip Sidney and John Keats.

Here are the basic rules of the dizain: 1) one 10-line stanza; 2) decasyllabic; 10 syllables per line; 3) rhymed ABABBCCDCD.

Double Sequidilla Sonnet —invented form:
The **Seguidilla** began as a popular dance song of Spain. The verse form was established and branched into variations by the 17th century. It has an alternating long short rhythm. The Seguidilla is: 1) stanzaic, written in any number of 2 part septets. (7 lines); 2) syllabic, 7-5-7-5 : 5-7-5 syllables per line, respectively. There is a slight pause between L4 and L5 suggesting L4 should be end-stopped; 3) rhymed usually by assonance XAXABXB or XAXABAB.,"X" representing an unrhymed line; 4) Full or True Rhyme is generally not used in favor of Assonantal echos; 5) composed with a *volta* or change in thought between L4 and L5.

Thus, the Sequidilla Sonnet consists of two of these septets.

Dramatic Monologue:
The Dramatic Monologue is not a fixed form of poetry. It depends on the mode of presentation and the apparent speaking voice. As the name suggests, the dramatic monologue presents a dramatic, "real-time" situation in which there is: 1) a single speaker, and 2) an implied auditor who never speaks in the poem, but whose actions or possible words are implied by

Dramatic Monologue (cont.)
the speaking voice. The great English poet, Robert Browning was the great master of the form, his most famous dramatic monologue being, undoubtedly, "My Last Duchess." (qv.).

Egyptian (Ancient) "Thought Couplets":
The verse pattern of rhymed and chiefly "closed" couplets is based upon a theoretical model of Ancient Egyptian prosody suggested by John L. Foster in an essay on "Thought Couplets" in Ancient Egyptian Verse." *Journal of Near Eastern Studies*, Jan. 1975, vol. 34, no. 1. University of Chicago]. There is no consistent us of "rhyming" in Ancient Eqyptian. Sonnet VII, "The time of Old Samhain draws nigh" (p. 8) was composed in this form.

Englyn Byr Cwca Sonnet (invented form):
Like the englyn cyrch, the *englyn byr cwca* is a Welsh form that uses both terminal and internal rhymes. The form: 1) comprised of tercets; 2) the first line has 7 syllables, the second has 10, and the third has 6; 3) lines 1 and 3 end rhyme with each other; 4) line 2 cross-rhymes with a syllable somewhere in the middle of the 3rd line. So: AXA BXB CXC etc. (where X is an unrhymed line in the tercet.), OR one might interlock the terets, as in Terza Rima. No rule against it! Thus: ABA BCB CDC etc.

Note: I have made the form into a sonnet by adding two 10-syllable lines following four Englyn Byr Cwca tercets.

French Sonnet:
The French sonnet, historially, appears after the Italian/Petrarchan sonnet. It commonly used iambic hexameters (Alexandrines) for its lines. The difference between the Italian and French forms is that, while the Italian rule of "never ending the poem with a rhymed couplet" was kept, the French form places a rhymed couplet at the beginning of the sestet. The Octave being the same as the Italian. The couplet of the sestet [CC] is followed by either DEED or DCDC or DEDE. Often the couplet is added to the octave with a line break preceding a final quatrain.

Gwawdodyn and the Gwawdodyn Sonnet (invented form):
The Gwawdodyn (gwow-dodin) is a Welsh four-line stanza of 9-9-10-9 syllables, rhyming AABA. The B-rhyme may rhyme with a syllable internally in the same line, OR, if the rhyme sound is prior to the final syllable, it cross- rhymes into the middle of the fourth line. I have done

the Gwawdodyn Sonnet by adding a nonosyllabic couplet after three
Gwawdodyns.

Haibun and Tanka Prose:
Traditionally, the Haibun is a blend of poetry and prose. Purists con-
sider the form to be a single Haiku poem (5-7-5 onji or syllable counts)
followed by a brief prose passage (often highly formal or even "purple")
on the same theme or topic. Tanka Prose is pretty much the same, but
with the poem used being a Tanka 5-7-5-7-7 instead of Haiku. It is the
present poet's opinion that much more could be done with this sort of
blendiing, allowing for several alternating poetry and prose passages.

Hir a Thoddaid / Hir a Thoddaid Sonnet (invented form):
Hir a Thoddaid is one of the Welsh official 24 meters. It is a 10-syllable
quatrain followed by a Thoddaid, which is a quatrain alternating between
10- and 9-syllable lines in which a syllable near the end of the 10-sylla-
ble first line rhymes into the middle of the following 9-syllable line; this
cross-rhyming is repeated in lines 3 and 4 of the quatrain. The 9-syllable
lines rhyme with each other. The initial quatrain is often monorhymed
AAAA, or slant rhymed AA₁A₂A₃, but this is not demanded. My version
of this type of sonnet leaves different schemes in the initial quatrains
open, but adds but a single final 10-9, rather than a full quatrain of
Thoddaid in order to create the **Hir a Thoddaid Sonnet** of 14 lines.

Japanese Sonnet (invented form):
The Japanese Sonnet is my coinage for the blending of three haiku and
one tanka, thus creating 14 lines using three three-syllable sections of
5-7-5 syllables and one section of 5-7-5-7-7 syllables. The tanka section
may be in ANY POSITION in the poem.

Kalevala Meter:
Elios Lonrot's collection of Finnish mythic and folkloric materials, *The
Kalevala*, has become universally recognized as the national epic of
the Finns. The meter is closely approximated in English using trochaic
tetrameter lines: /u/u/u/u. Traditionally, Finnish "rune singers" would
sit opposite one another, clasp hands, and, rocking back and forth, chant
out verses. The initiator of a verse is echoed in a paraphrased line by the
second chanter.

Kashmiri Vakh Sonnet (invented form):
The elements of the Kashmiri Vakh are: 1) a tetrastich, a poem in 4

Kashmiri Vakh Sonnet (cont.)
lines—occasionally two stanzas of 4 lines; 2) syllabic, lines of 7 syllables each, with the additional requirement of 4 stresses per line [NOTE: These accents may fall in any positions in the seven syllables of the line.]; 3) optional ABAB alternate rhyme with either true or near rhyme. I have added a couplet following three Vakh quatrains/tetrastiches.

Korean Kasa and Korean Kasa Sonnet (invented form):
The Korean Kasa is usually octasyllabic The unusual thing about the form is the use of "Head Rhymes" (the first words of lines rhyme, rather than the final words)—usually in groups of two lines (head-rhymed couplets), but can be extended over several lines. The "echoes" may be instances of *consonance* rather than full rhyme. Usually, the line is broken 4 and 4 syllables with a caesura or shift. The poem can be heptasyllabic, in which case it is head-rhymed or consonated as above, except then broken into 3, then 4 syllable groups. I have made a *Korean Kasa Sonnet* by using seven head-rhymed couplets.

Ljothahattr ("Song Measure"):
Lyothahattr is an Old Norse accentual meter counting 4-3-4-3 accents, "four-three measure" in quatrains. The criteria: Lines one and three are in the "four-four measure" of traditional *Fornythislag*. These lines have all the same structure, each line being sharply divided by a cæsural pause into two half-lines, and each half-line having two accented syllables and two (sometimes three) unaccented ones. The two half lines are bound by alliteration across the caesura by three (2-1) or sometimes (1-1) accented syllables. Lines two and four are shorter, have no cæsural pause, have only three accented syllables, and regularly two alliterated and accented syllables.

Middle English "Thirteener":
Middle English *thirteener*, is a verse form with thirteen lines rhymed ABABABABcDDDC. Sonnet X on page 11, "Nearing All Hallows" is a "Thirteener" composed in heptasyllabics, BUT as indicated by the lower-case "c" in the rhyme scheme, the first "C" rhyme is a shorter line (4 syllables in this case). Yes, it's not technically a "sonnet," but I include it in the sequence as a form very close to the sonnet. The first eight lines are in the scheme of the Sicilian Octave of the earliest sonnets.

Octfochlach and Octfochlach Sonnet (invented form):
The Ochtfochlach is a Irish form from the 13th century. Unlike
many of the more complicated *dán díreach* or strict Irish forms
the Ochtfochlach uses simpler rhymes and is less formal in struc-
ture. Considered *óglachas* or "apprentice work", it was often used by
novices.

The elements of the Ochtfochlach are: 1) an octastich, a poem
in 8 lines; 2) it is syllabic, *with syllable counts at the discretion of the
poet* as long as the lines are uniform length; 3) it is rhymed, AAAB-
CCCB. I have truncated the form with a final sestet (rather than
octave), rhymed DDEFFE to complete a 14-line poem.

Pararhyme:
Pararhyme is a particular type of *Slant Rhyme* or *Near Rhyme* (occasion-
ally called *Off Rhyme*) in which echoing consonant sounds both begin
and end the rhyming words—with ONLY the medial vowel changing.
Poet Wilfred Owen was a particular champion and experimenter with
this form in works such as "Arms and the Boy" and "Futility." Examples of
pararhymes: *bleed : blood : bled : blade* and *star : stir : steer : stair : store.* It
also works well when combined with more traditional slant rhyming.

Pie Quebrado Sonnet (invented form):
Pie quebrado (Spanish for "broken foot" or "limping verse") is a
short line that follows longer lines as a sort of "tail." Usually, a
four-syllable line follows a couplet of eight-syllable lines.
I have used two six-line groups rhyming: AABCCB and DDEFFE
and a couplet GG [my addition of the couplet to make the total 14
lines for the sonnet], with syllable counts of 884884 | 884884 | 88.

Quatranelle (invented form):
The Quatranelle is based upon the Terzanelle (itself a "blending" of terza
rima and the villanelle forms). Instead of terza rima tercets, in the Qua-
tranelle I have used an interlocking rubaiyat stanza as the base. In this
pattern, the third line of the rubái is unrhymed with the other three, but
it carries over as the main rhyme of each subsequent quatrain.

The subscripted rhymes A_1 and A_2 are the two main refrains which re-
peat (or slightly paraphrase) in the five-line envoi. The rhymes with sub-
scripted $_R$ indicate lines that are initiated in one stanza, but then repeated
(or slightly paraphrased) as the last line of the subsequent stanza.

I have also expanded the terzanelle number of stanzas (six, including
the four-line envoi) by the 4/3[rds] difference between the tercet and the

Quatranelle (cont.)
quatrain, thus ending with an eight-stanza pattern (including the five-line envoi).

$$A_1AB_RA_2$$
$$BBC_RB_R$$
$$CCD_RC_R$$
$$DDE_RD_R$$
$$EEF_RE_R$$
$$FFG_RF_R$$
$$GGH_RG_R$$

$$HHA_1H_RA_2$$

Rannaicheacht Ghairid:
(ron-a'yach cha'r-rid) [versification with "clipped" or shortened line]

The elements or this Irish form are: 1) written in any number of quatrains with uneven lines; 2) syllabic in lines of 3-7-7-7syllables; 3)ideally, at least 2 words alliterate in each line; 4) rhymed AABA, with the end word of L3 cross-rhymed into the first half or L4.

x x a

x x x x x x a

x x x x x x b

x x b x x x a.

Rondel Supreme / Rondel Supreme Sonnet—(invented form):
Rondel Supreme/or Rondel Prime Abba abAB abbaAB where the capital letters represent repeated refrain lines. French 13th c. [rondel="little round"]. There are no restrictions on line length or meter, although many were written in Alexandrines. Since it's a quatorzain, a "fourteener," why not use it as a sonnet?

Rubáiyát Sonnet:
Edward FitzGerald's famous translation of *The Rubáiyát of Omar Khayyám*, although being quite widely known, does not carry with it the general awareness of WHY the poem is a Rubáiyát. A Rubáiyát is a poem composed in quatrains called *Rubái*. The rhyme scheme of a Rubái stanza is AABA. The Rubáiyát Sonnet is a poem comprised of three interlocking Rubái and a rhymed couplet: AABA BBCB CCDC DD. Note that the poem is "interlocked" because the unrhymed line from one quatrain becomes the main rhyme of the succeeding quatrain.

Rupert Brooke Sonnet:
Rupert Brooke, one of the British WWI poets who died in the war, left
us the wonderful and famous sonnet "The Soldier," which begins: "If I
should die, think only this of me: / That there's some corner of a foreign
field / That is forever England…." The poem rhymes in a distinctive
pattern that is a blend of English and Italian forms, having an "octave" in
English-style alternating quatrains: ABABCDCD and a "sestet" follow-
ing the traditional Italian ending of EFGEFG.

Rhupunt / Rhupunt Sonnet (invented form):
The Rhupunt is one of the 24 official Welsh meters. As with most of these,
it is rather difficult to write in English due to the large number of internal
rhymes needed. It is a line (not a stanza) of three, four, or five sections of four
syllables each. Whatever line length is chosen— 12, 16, or 20 syllables—all
sections of four, except for the last must rhyme on the fourth syllable. The last
section of four syllables carries the main rhyme. The 12-syllable form approx-
imates the accentual-syllabic Alexandrine. Thus, a Rhupunt sonnet, although
extremely difficul to rhyme in English, may be of various line lengths and
rhyme schemes, so long as it fits the rules for internal and terminal rhyming
and is fourteen lines long.

Seadna (shay-na):
This Irish form is quite difficult and almost impossible to replicate in English.
The basic requir4ements of the form: 1) quatrains of 8-7-8-7 syllables; 2)
Lines 1 and 3 end on 2-syllable words; 3) Lines 2 and 4 end on 1-syllable
words; 4) Lines 2 and 4 end-rhyme

   The more difficult requirements of the form: A) every line has alliter-
ation; B) the final syllable of line 1 alliterates with a stressed word of line
2; C) Line 3 rhymes with the penultimate word of line 4

   I have striven to come close to this pattern in "The Dulachan" p. 140.

Seguidilla / Double Sequidilla Sonnet —invented form:
The Seguidilla began as a popular dance song of Spain. The verse form was
established and branched into variations by the 17th century. It has an alter-
nating long short rhythm.

   The Seguidilla is: 1) stanzaic, written in any number of 2 part septets. (7
lines); 2) syllabic, 7-5-7-5 : 5-7-5 per line. There is a slight pause between L4
and L5 suggesting L4 should be end-stopped; 3) rhymed usually by assonance
xaxabxb or xaxabab. x being unrhymed. <u>True rhyme is generally not used</u>; 4)
composed with a volta or change in thought between L4 and L5.
Thus, the **Sequidilla Sonnet** consists of two of these septets.

Sestinelle (invented form):

The Sestinelle is an extrapolated hybrid form based upon the traditional Villanelle and Sestina.

Like the Sestina, the hexains of the poem shift in a rearrangement of the final words or terminal rhyme sounds of the six stanzas in the following manner: 123456, 615243, 364125, 532614, 451362, 246531. At that point, the Sestinelle differs from the Sestina in that a seventh hexain is added, repeating the 123456 word or rhyme sound numbers.

Like the Villanelle, the Sestinelle uses refrains (optionally Full Refrains (fully repeated lines), Partial Refrains (as the word suggests), Incremental Refrains (paraphrases of repeated lines) or any combination thereof. These refrains are set up as follows [NOTE: the letter R following a number indicates the refrain pattern]: 123456R, 6R15243R, 3R64125R, 5R32614R, 4R51362R, 2R46531R, 1R23456R.

At this point, a distinction between a Rhymed and an Unrhymed Sestinelle is needed.

In the Unrhymed form, as with the Sestina, there are six different words [or in this case, optionally, rhyme sounds] which are then repeated in the order as noted above.

In the Rhymed form, either two or three rhyme sounds are used. If two rhyme sounds are used, then the pattern begins ABABAB in the initial hexain, with the second hexain rhyming BAABBA, etc. If three rhyme sounds are used, then the pattern of rhymes in the first hexain is either ABCABC, followed by CABBAC, etc. OR, with an initial hexain of ABCCBA, which is followed by AABBCC, etc. [as has been used in the poem "Katabasis" (pages 134-135).

The *Envoi* of the Rhymed Sestinelle concludes the poem with three internally rhymed lines in either order: AA | BB | CC or CC | BB | AA (as in "Katabasis").

The Envoi of the Unrhymed Sestinelle [as in the "Extended Sestinelle" titled "Cursed Mansion" on pages 135-137] is different. In two hexadecimal lines, the final words or rhyme sounds of whatever comprises the final hexain are repeated in reverse order. In the Standard Sestinelle of seven hexains, this would result in two long lines: xxx6xxx5xxx4 and xxx3xxx2xxx1 [where the Xs represent ANY SYLLABLE and the numbers represent the words or rhyme sounds that have been used for those numbers in the hexains of the poem.

The Extended Sestinelle is simply a poem in this repetition and shuffling of words or rhyme sounds that goes beyond the normal seven hexains. In such as case (as in "Cursed Mansion"), whatever the final hexain pattern is is repeated in the long hexameter lines in the reverse order of the ending words or sounds of the final hexain.

"Similance" (my coinage):
I define "Similance" as "the noticeable repetition of similar sounds in prox-
imate words." It might also be called "Slant Consonance," since it is based
upon the realization that consonant sounds in our language (and others)
can be grouped as pairs—Voiced or Unvoiced versions of, in effect, the
same sound. A consonant is *voiced* if there is vibration in the vocal chords
upon its pronunciation. It is *unvoiced*, if there is no such vibration. Thus,
we have the following PAIRS that can provide a pleasing "Similance"
when heard in proximity [the Voiced is first, the Unvoiced second in most
examples in this series]: BP / DT / VF / GK / LR (both can be voiced) /
MN (the "humms" both voiced / ZS / ZH SH. Words using these pairs
in noticeable proximity sound good together.

Slant / Near / Off Rhyme:
Whereas Full or True Rhyme is the exact repetition of the final vowel
sound of a syllable or word and any succeeding consonant sounds, Slant
Rhyme is usually the repetition of different vowel sounds before the same
final consonant of a syllable: *hit, sat, put, great, lot*, etc. It can be done with
vocalic (final vowel only) rhymes in that all syllables ending with vowel
sounds Slant Rhyme with all other syllables ending in any other vowel
sound. This differs from other echoing techniques (*Rhyme* in its broad-
est sense being "the noticeable repetition of exact or similar sounds in
words"), such as *Alliteration* (the noticeable repetition of initial sounds of
proximate words) and *Consonance* (the noticeable repetition if medial or
terminal consonant sounds in proximate words).

Sonnets—General History and My Invented Forms:
In addition to the 72-title opening sonnet sequence "What the Night
Brings & Other Sonnets," this book includes many other poems in the
form of the quatorzain—a great many of them are experimental hybrid
forms, making use of poetic froms from many nationalities, cultures, and
epochs, from Classical through Medieval and Renaissance do modern
forms.

 In addition, many of the poems included are forms invented by the
present poet, making use of irregular divisions and/or rhyming patterns.

 Assuming that most readers will be familiar with the two most com-
monly seen sonnet forms used in English: the Italian or Petrarchan form
and the English or Shakespearean form, I have not labeled in the formal
credits below these poems Italian/Petrarchan or English/Shakespearean
as such—assuming the likely familiarity of most readers.

 What most readers will not be aware of is the fact that the Italian **Son-**

form, attributed by name to Francesco Petrarca (Petrarch [1304-1374]), was not invented or first used by Petrarch. And others: Dante [Alighieri 1265-1321] and Michaelangelo [Buonarroti 1475-1564] to name two, also used the rhyme abbaabba cdcdcd OR cdecde in an octave and sestet division. The real originator of the sonnet form is generally agreed to have been Giacomo da Lentini [fl. 13th c.] who developed the sonnet from the older form of the strambotto and made use of the Sicilian Octave [abababab] rather than the Italian Octave [abbaabba].

To call the "English" form by the name "Shakepearean" is also a misnomer, since Shakepeare did not invent the rhyme pattern, but merely used it famously in his 154 sonnets. Credit for what has come to us as the English Sonnet belongs to Henry Howard, Earl of Surrey [1516-1547], who simplified the sonnet for the more "rhyme-poor" language of English (our language has dropped most of its case endings, resulting for more difficulties in finding good rhymes). Surrey's division of the sonnet into three Italian Quatrains and a concluding rhymed couplet (abab cdcd efef gg) requires the poet to only need one rhyming line for any other single line. The Italian form requires 4As, 4Bs, and often 3Cs and 3Ds.

Now, as to the sonnets in this collection. The "hybrid" sonnets, made by adapting various cultural, national, and specific historical patterns from many languages into fourteen-line poems (the ONLY requirement the current poet has for labeling a poem "a sonnet")—these are handled in this glossary by the name of the exotic pattern beiing adapted and adopted.

The following are experiments and inventions of sonnets that are also to be found in this collection:

*The 4-6-4 Sonnet is any sonnet so divided on the page, making use of two quatrains surrounding a central hexain or sestet of lines. The quatrains may be Italian Quatrains (XYYX as in the example sonnet XXII), or may be Sicilian Quatrains [XYXY], or may be Rubiyat Quatrains [XXYX], or may be any two of these various types used to open and close the poem. The central section of six lines may be an Envelope Hexain [XYZZYX], a Repeated Tercet Hexain [XYZXYZ (as in sonnet XXII), or a Repeated Unrhymed Couplet Hexain [XYXYXY]. Thus, a great many options, but all fulfilling the 4-5-4 overall scheme.

*The Quatrain-Couplet Blend Sonnet is any combination of two quatrains and three couplets and in any order, with the exception that both quatrains cannot be consecutive. Thus, a pattern of 2-4-2-4-2, or 2-4-2-2-4, or 2-2-4-2-4, or 4-2-4-2-2, or 4-2-2-2-4 are all acceptable. The couplets are rhymed couplets; the quatrains can be Italian ABBA, Sicilian

ABAB, Rubaiyat AABA, or Ballad ABCB, or any two of these forms used. Again,—very flexible. Breaks between sections are also arbitrary, depending on the purposes and designs of the poet.

*The 6-2-6 Sonnet is a sonnet, as the numbers suggest, with a rhymed couplet between two hexains. The hexains/sestets may be in any of the following patterns: XYXYXY (Sicilian Sestet); XYZXYZ (one form of the Italian Sestet); or XYZZYX (Envelope Sestet). The poem can be divided into any pattern of lines or sections.

*The 5-5-4 Sonnet (invented form):
This sonnet is two pentains/pentastiches followed by a quatrain. The two five-line initial segments rhyme either ABCBA ABCBA or ABCBA DECED. The quatrain may be in any form.

*The 5-3-4-2 Sonnet is based upon the numbers of accents in three consecutive quatrains (rhymed in any scheme) and concluding with a pentameter/5-accented-syllable couplet. Thus, accentually, the poem's pattern is 5-3-4-2 | 5-3-4-2 | 5-3-4-2 | 5-5 in either accentual or accentual-syllabic measures (with the foot used, if accentual-syllabic, being optional: iambic, anapestic, trochaic, or dactylic (or any of these with metrical variation).

The Telesillean line is an acephalous ("headless") version of the Glyconic line (x)//uu/u/ — where x is either a long or accented or short or unaccented syllable. The form is named after and was used by Tellesilla, a poetess of Argos (5th c. B.C.).

Thus, this version (also known as the *Telesillean*—Latin: *telesilleus*), is (In modern English poetics [qualitative accentual-syllabic meter, rather than the Classical "quantitative" measures of long or short syllables], the custom is to replace longs with stressed syllables and shorts with unstressed syllables. Thus, one form of the accentual-syllabic *telesillean* would run: / / uu / u / (in other terms, a spondee, an anapest, and an iamb).

Terzanelle Le Grande [and Terzanelle Majeure] (invented forms):
These forms are my expansions of the traditional Terzanelle—itself a hybrid of the Villanelle and Terza Rima, displaying characteristics of both.

The traditional Terzanelle is a 19-line poem comprised of five interlocked tercets (terza rima), but using extra refrain lines carried from one tercet to the next, with the unrhymed central line of the each tercet repeated (or paraphrased) as the final line of the subsequent tercet. The first and third lines of the initial tercet become lines used as refrains in a concluding four-line envoi: A1BA2 | bCB | cDC | dED | eFE | fA1FA2 where A1 and A2 are the primary refrains and the Capital Letters Repre

Terzanelle Le Grande [and Terzanelle Majeure] (cont.)
sent lines repeated or parphrased in the final line of the following tercet.
And optional Envoi rhyme is fFA1A2

The Terzanelle Le Grande uses 15 stanzas in this same pattern followed
by a similarly formed four-line envoi.

The Terzanelle Majeure is comprised of 10 stanzas in this same pattern
followed by a similarly formed four-line envoi.

Trisengraf (invented form):
William Carlos Williams wrote many of his poems using the "free verse
form" that he called the "Triversen" (Three-Verse Sentence), separating
the sentence into three lines, usually in phrases or clauses. My "Trisen-
graf" is a "Three Sentence Paragraph" comprised of three Triversens. This
is about as close as I come to using vers libre.

Verso Pareado and Verso Pareado Sonnet—the latter, invented form:
Verso Pareado is a Spanish form of the 14th and 15th centuries. Simply
put, it consists in rhymed couplets in hendecasyallabic (11-syllable) lines.
I have used seven of these couplets to make the **Verso Pareado Sonnet.**

Villanelle:
The Villanelle is one of the Fixed French Forms consisting of five three-
line stanzas and a final quatrain, with the first and third lines of the first
stanza repeating alternately in the following stanzas. These two refrain
lines form the final couplet in the quatrain. See "Do Not Go Gentle into
That Good Night" by Dylan Thomas, Elizabeth Bishop's "One Art," and
Edwin Arlington Robinson's "The House on the Hill." The rhyme scheme
is: A1 b A2 / a b A1 / a b A2 / a b A1 / a b A2 / a b A1 A2 where A1
and A2 are the repetons (refrain lines—usually repeated exactly, but
some poets have used partial or incrementally paraphrased refrains.

Acknowledgements

"A Cabin in the Wood" first appeared in *Spectral Realms #19*, Summer 2023. ed. S. T. Joshi. New York: Hippocampus Press.. 2023.

"The Clingers" first appeared in *Spectral Realms #16*, Winter 2022. ed. S. T. Joshi. New York: Hippocampus Press, 2022.

"The Collection" first appeared in *The Horror Zine Magazine*, Spring 2022.

"Crossing Over" first appeared in Liquid Imagination #52, Fall 2022. https://liquidimagination.silverpen.org/article/crossing-over-by-frank-coffman/

"The Dreamer and the Dreaded Ones" first appeared in *For the Outsider: Poems Inspired by H. P. Lovecraft*. ed. S. T. Joshi. New York: Hippocampus Press, 2023.

"Eidolon Tetratych" first appeared in *Spectral Realms #16*, Winter 2022. ed. S. T. Joshi. New York: Hippocampus Press, 2022.

"Figures of Shadow" first appeared in *A Walk in a City of Shadows: Tales of Urban Legendry*. ed. Sarah Walker, Gordon B. White, Phil Breach, Nora B. Peevy, and Jill Hand. Alien Sun Press, 2022.

"Hr's Gonna Find Out" first appeared in *Horrifying Holidays: Holiday Spookfest*. ed. Gary Hill. Rockford, IL: Tales of Wonder and Dread Publishing, 2021.

"I See Too Much" first appeared in *Spectral Realms #17*, Summer 2022. ed. S. T. Joshi. New York: Hippocampus Press, 2022.

"The Kannibaali" first appeared in *Penumbra #3, 2022*. ed. S. T. Joshi. New York: Hippocampus Press, 2022.

"Lob" first appeared in *Spectral Realms #19*, Summer 2023. ed. S. T. Joshi. New York: Hippocampus Press, 2023.

"Locus Horroris" first appeared in *Spectral Realms #18*, Winter 2023. ed. S. T. Joshi. New York: Hippocampus Press, 2023.

"The Lorelei" first appeared in *Spectral Realms #16*, Winter 2022. ed. S. T. Joshi. New York: Hippocampus Press, 2022.

"Pareidolia?" first appeared leading off the 12-16-2022 Blog Posting from Timber Ghost Press, edited by Cody Langille. timberghostpress. com

"Pericula Noctis"" first appeared in *Spectral Realms #18*, Winter 2023. ed. S. T. Joshi. New York: Hippocampus Press, 2023.

"The Seeker's Lament" first appeared in *Spectral Realms #17*, Summer 2022. ed. S. T. Joshi. New York: Hippocampus Press, 2022.

"Skinner" first appeared in *The Horror Zine Magazine*, Spring 2022.

"Strange Door, Odd Key" first appeared in *Spectral Realms #19*, Summer 2023. ed. S. T. Joshi. New York: Hippocampus Press, 2023.

"Veniat ei Malum qui Vocat Malum" first appeared in *For the Outsider: Poems Inspired by H. P. Lovecraft*. ed. S. T. Joshi. New York: Hippocampus Press, 2023.

"We Only Know a Name" first appeared as "Mr. Illusive" in *Spectral Realms #18*, Winter 2023. ed. S. T. Joshi. New York: Hippocampus Press, 2023.

"When the Suns Set Over Carcosa" first appeared in *Forbidden Knowledge, Cyäegha Special Publication #10*, 2022

COLOPHON

The basic text used is Adobe Jenson Pro
11 on stanardized leading of 13.2 pts.
Titles are in Bold Adobe Jenson Pro 12 pt.
Epigraphs and Notes on Forms and Types are in 10 pt.

The Book's Title is done in an artistic style
by Paul "Mutartis" Boswell and is not a standard font.

The Sonnet Sequence
Part 1 and the Other Poems Part 3
are headed by TheGhhost font

PART III THE KIMI XIBALBA
IS HEADED BY AMBAGES FONT

PART IV GHOSTS OF THE FOX VALLEY
IS HEADED BY PHANTOM GHOST FONT

Part V Poems of Science Fiction
is headed by Bauhaus 93

PART VI POLITICAL POEMS
IS HEADED BY STARS AND STRIPES

Part VII is headed by Adobe Jenson Bold